Sugarcraft MODELLING

Sugarcraft MODELLING

STEPHEN BENISON

MEREHURST

To Karina, Laura and Ashley, my three most-important treasures –
you now have my undivided attention.

With Thanks
To my family and friends for your loyal interest. To Clarice Tadd for your help with the cake
preparation, and Bob and Carol Peilow of Cake Art for your continued support.

A big thank you to the behind-the-scenes team: Clive Streeter for your patience with the fine details;
Jo Tapper for your creative expertise; and last, but not least, to Bridget Jones whose humour and
enthusiasm has kept me going through the long months of compiling this book. Thank you team.

The author and publishers would like to thank the following for their help.
Anniversary House (Cake Decorations) Ltd., Unit 16, Elliott Road, West Howe Industrial Estate,
Bournemouth, BH11 8LZ;
Cake Art Ltd., Venture Way, Crown Industrial Estate, Priorswood, Taunton, Somerset, TA2 8DE;
Floradesac, 53 Woodcock Industrial Estate, Warminster, Wiltshire, BA12 9DX;
Guy, Paul and Co. Ltd., Unit B4, Foundry Way, Little End Road, Eaton Socon, Cambs., PE19 3JH
J.F. Renshaw Ltd., Crown Street, Liverpool, L8 7RF for all marzipan and sugarpaste used in this title;
Orchard Products, 51 Hallyburton Road, Hove, East Sussex, BN3 7GP; and
Squires Kitchen, Squires House, 3 Waverley Lane, Farnham, Surrey, GU9 8BB.

Published in 1995 by Merehurst Limited, Ferry House, 51-57 Lacy Road, Putney,
London SW15 1PR

Designed by Jo Tapper
Edited by Bridget Jones
Photography by Clive Streeter
Colour separation by P & W Graphics Pte Ltd, Singapore
Printed by Wing King Tong, Hong Kong

NOTES ON USING THE RECIPES
For all recipes, quantities are given in metric, Imperial and cup measurements. Follow one set of
measurements only as they are not interchangeable. Standard 5ml teaspoons (tsp) and 15ml
tablespoons (tbsp) are used. Australian readers, whose tablespoons measure 20ml, should adjust
quantities accordingly. All spoon measures are assumed to be level unless otherwise stated.
Eggs are a standard size 3 (medium) unless otherwise stated.

CONTENTS

INTRODUCTION

Modelling takes many forms in a variety of mediums but whatever the particular art or craft, it is often everyday items that provide the inspiration for the work. People, animals, scenery, flowers and objects are all typical subjects that provide a simple starting point from which many styles can emerge according to the skill, culture and opinions of the artist. Whether the model is created in a sugar medium or sculpting material, the spirit of the idea comes from the first attraction that stirs up the desire to interpret the theme.

There are three key approaches to modelling. Firstly, it can be a means of construction, using patterns and templates literally to build up the piece by assembling various carefully made parts. Alternatively, moulds can be used to give the paste structure which can be further modelled into a more personal form. Using moulds is particularly useful for making several pieces that are the same or similar as it saves a great deal of time.

Hand modelling is the other main method. Unlike the construction or moulding techniques, here the paste is manipulated into shape to resemble the subject and this freestyle approach evolves as the skills of the modeller develop. People and animals can be animated and given individual characters to fit in with the theme or to please the recipient.

Within this range of techniques, different sugar mediums can be used to make models ranging from small, basic items to intricate pieces of work demanding a high-level of expertise and skill. In compiling this book, I have drawn on many years of experience and experimentation to bring together examples of sugar modelling that are intended to enthuse the novice as well as those who are confident with sugarcraft. The chapters explore the different sugar mediums which can be used to make decorations for cakes or freestanding models, and the majority are linked to some occasion or celebration.

Teaching and learning skills like modelling are closely linked and I find both a great source of enjoyment. Whenever you need an honest opinion on your endeavours, remember that children are always ready with a true – if sometimes rather blunt – comment. My children, Laura and Ashley, and wife, Karina, are my most valued critics – I know they are honest, not polite, and many of the projects in the pages that follow came together thanks to their input. So when you are engrossed in modelling a cat and a young observer comments on your rabbit, you know it is time to start again! I hope you will find this book both useful and fun to follow, and that it will give you and the recipient of your modelling many hours of pleasure.

PASTES FOR MODELLING

Pastillage

I include two recipes – if you already have some experience of modelling with sugar, you may have your own favourite recipe which you may prefer to use. Each paste has a different texture and a preferred application depending on the ingredients it contains.

Pastillage 1

This is a gelatine paste which is ideal for flat-piece constructions and plaques. It does not shrink back too much when rolled out.

15ml (1 tablespoon) gelatine
60ml (2 fl oz/¼ cup) water
5 ml (1 teaspoon) liquid glucose (clear corn syrup)
5 ml (1 teaspoon) white vegetable fat (shortening)
2 drops of lemon juice
440g (14 oz/2½ cups) icing (confectioners') sugar
15 ml (1 tablespoon) albumen powder
60g (2 oz/½ cup) cornflour (cornstarch)

Sprinkle the gelatine over the water and leave to stand for 15 minutes until spongy. Place over a saucepan of barely simmering water and stir until the gelatine has dissolved. Turn the heat off under the pan. Add the liquid glucose and white fat to the dissolved gelatine and stir until the fat has melted and the ingredients combined. Remove the bowl from the pan of hot water. Mix in the lemon juice.

Place half the icing sugar in the bowl of a large electric food mixer and add the albumen powder. Pour in the gelatine mixture and mix on slow speed using the beater attachment until the mixture is white. Gradually add the remaining icing sugar and the cornflour, beating on slow speed until each addition is mixed.

Turn out onto a surface lightly dusted with icing sugar and knead until firm. Cut into four pieces and wrap each in a polythene bag. Place in an airtight container and leave in the refrigerator for 24 hours. Knead well before use.

MODELLING MEMO

After chilling, the pastillage may be warmed in the microwave for 5 seconds, reducing the amount of kneading required to soften the paste. This paste freezes well for long periods; it should be thawed overnight in the refrigerator, then kneaded until warm and pliable.

Pastillage 2

This gives a very white, smooth paste which stretches a little but does not shrink back quite as much after rolling out as in recipe 1. It is ideal for all types of modelling.

10ml (2 teaspoons) white vegetable fat (shortening)
5ml (1 teaspoon) liquid glucose (clear corn syrup)
500g (1 lb) royal icing
15ml (1 tablespoon) gum tragacanth
170g (5½ oz/1 cup) icing (confectioners') sugar

Place the fat and liquid glucose in a heatproof bowl over a saucepan of simmering water and stir occasionally until well combined.

Place the royal icing in a mixing bowl. Add the gum tragacanth and melted mixture, then mix to form a firm paste. Gradually add the icing sugar. Knead the paste until it is smooth and elastic. Cut the paste into quarters and place each portion in a polythene bag. Store the wrapped paste in an airtight container in the refrigerator for 24 hours before use. This paste can also be frozen.

Modelling Paste

A mixture of equal quantities of flower paste and sugarpaste, this dries hard but the sugarpaste slows the drying, allowing more time for modelling. Modelling paste should be made from matured flower paste.

Flower Paste

This quick paste is suitable for fine modelling as it can be rolled translucently thin; it also remains workable for a longer period than the other pastes, allowing time to model intricate items.

5ml (1 teaspoon) white vegetable fat (shortening)
5ml (1 teaspoon) liquid glucose (clear corn syrup)
250g (8 oz) royal icing
30ml (2 tablespoons) carboxymethyl cellulose or Tylose powder

Place the fat and liquid glucose in a heat-proof bowl over a saucepan of simmering water and stir occasionally until well combined.

Place the royal icing in a bowl, then add the carboxymethyl cellulose or Tylose. Pour in the melted mixture and mix the ingredients into a firm paste. Turn the paste out onto a surface lightly dusted with icing sugar and knead it until it begins to feel elastic.

Cut the paste into small pieces and coat each piece with a little white vegetable fat. Place in a polythene bag in an airtight container and store in the refrigerator for 24 hours to allow the paste to mature. Knead well before using.

Rock Sugar

500g (1 lb/2 cups) granulated (crystalline) sugar
125ml (4 fl oz/½ cup) water
30g (1 oz) royal icing

Line a large ovenproof bowl with foil. Have a sugar thermometer ready, warming in a bowl of hot water, as well as cold water in the sink or a suitable bowl for cooling the base of the saucepan when the syrup has cooked.

Place the sugar and water in a heavy-bottomed saucepan. Heat, stirring occasionally and very gently, until the sugar dissolves. Stop stirring and bring the syrup to the boil.

Remove the scum from the surface of the syrup with a metal tea strainer but do not stir the syrup at all. Rinse the inside of the saucepan by running a little water down off a pastry brush. This dissolves any sugar crystals which may be forming above the line of the syrup on the side of the saucepan. Once crystals begin to form, or if the syrup is stirred at all once it boils, the sugar will crystalize before the syrup has boiled sufficiently.

Continue boiling until the syrup reaches 138°C (280°F) on a sugar thermometer. Then arrest the cooking process by immersing the base of the saucepan in cold water. Be quick so that the syrup does not overcook and remove the pan promptly from the water to prevent the syrup cooling too much.

Immediately stir in the royal icing, then pour the mixture into the prepared bowl. Mixing the cold royal icing with the hot sugar creates steam and puffs the sugar mixture into rock-like shapes. Allow the rock sugar to cool before breaking off pieces which can be sprayed with different food colourings or used as required.

Royal Icing

22g (¾ oz/9 teaspoons) albumen powder
155ml (5 fl oz/⅔ cup) warm water
875g (1/¾ lb/5¼ cups) icing
    (confectioners') sugar, sifted

Mix the albumen and water, and leave it to stand for 15 minutes. Strain the albumen into the grease-free bowl of an electric mixer, then add two-thirds of the icing sugar and beat on slow speed for 3 minutes. Add the remaining icing sugar and continue to beat for a further 2 minutes, until the

icing is glossy and it stands in soft peaks. Adjust the consistency with a little water if required.

Sugar Glue

Place a piece of sugarpaste about the size of a walnut in a saucepan. Add 30ml (2 tablespoons) boiled water and heat gently, stirring to break up the sugarpaste, then bring to the boil. Cool before using. For a slightly stronger glue use pastillage not sugarpaste.

Marzipan

There are many different brands of marzipans; the best is made from ground almonds, sugar and liquid glucose (clear corn syrup). The proportions of these ingredients vary according to cost and the recommended use for the paste. In order that the product can be called marzipan, it has to conform to requirements in terms of the proportions of almonds and sugar used. There are also other types of nut-based modelling pastes but they are not suitable for all the marzipan models.

A white base marzipan has been used for all the models in this book. If you find that the marzipan you are using for modelling is a little too soft, work more icing (confectioners') sugar into it. The raw base marzipan can be obtained from a baker or confectionery supplier and it is the best paste for larger models as it readily takes up extra icing sugar if necessary, giving a choice of a soft or slightly firmer paste.

Adding a little gum tragacanth to the marzipan will set it, allowing for more difficult shapes to be moulded. I use 5ml (1 teaspoon) gum tragacanth to each 250g (8 oz) marzipan. Knead the gum tragacanth into the paste, then use it straight away - by the time the marzipan is modelled, the gum will begin to set. Prepare only enough marzipan for use within 24 hours;

once the gum tragacanth is added, if the marzipan is left any longer, it becomes tight and oily when worked.

Finally, pay attention to hygiene when modelling and remember that you are working with an edible medium. Keeping tools and surfaces spotlessly clean is not only important for food safety, it will ensure that the modelled items have a fresh finish.

Modelling Marzipan

280g (9 oz) liquid glucose (clear corn
    syrup)
1.5kg (3 lb) raw marzipan
1.25kg (2½ lb) icing (confectioners')
    sugar

Warm the liquid glucose in a heavy-bottomed saucepan over low heat until it is runny. Break up the marzipan and place it in the bowl of a large food mixer. Use the beater attachment – not the whisk – to blend the warmed liquid glucose into the marzipan. If you do not have a large food mixer, then place the marzipan and liquid glucose in a large bowl and mix until thoroughly combined.

Gradually add the icing sugar, until the paste is soft and smooth, without any traces of icing sugar. Place the marzipan in a thick polythene bag and store it in an airtight container in a cool place.

It is best to leave the marzipan to stand for 24 hours to firm up before use. The marzipan will keep well for several months if it is tightly wrapped and kept in an airtight container in a cool place but not in the refrigerator. If it is not well wrapped, it will form a crust. Any dried marzipan must be cut away, otherwise small particles of crust will be mixed into the paste, making it lumpy.

If you are unable to obtain raw marzipan, use good-quality white marzipan and add a little icing sugar if it is too soft.

Problems with Pastillage

Simple problems can cause disappointing results when using pastillage; many are easily avoided or solved.

Small specks of gelatine appear in paste

◆ Place the paste in a polythene bag in a bowl over a pan of simmering water for 10 minutes. Knead well, until smooth and free of specks.

Paste is short and crumbly

◆ Add a little water or beaten egg white. Work a small amount of white vegetable fat (shortening) onto your hands then knead the paste.

Skin appears on paste surface after rolling out

◆ Avoid rolling in a draught or near an open window.
◆ Do not roll out too much paste at once.
◆ Keep paste covered when not in use.

Paste sticks to rolling board

◆ Dust the surface of the board with cornflour dusting bag.

Drag lines appear on paste when cutting out

◆ Knife or scalpel blade not sharp or coated with dried pastillage.
◆ Use a chopping action to cut the pastillage if using a knife.
◆ Cut towards yourself if using a scalpel.
◆ Use a long cutting blade held at a 45° angle to the pastillage.

Paste shrinks back after cutting

◆ Roll out the pastillage to the required thickness, then cover with a thin sheet of polythene and allow the paste to rest before cutting.

Surface of paste feels sugary

◆ Icing (confectioners') sugar used on surface – use only cornflour (corn starch) to dust the surface.
◆ Polish the surface of the pastillage with a smoother before cutting out to give a silky smooth finish.

Cut out shape distorts after cutting

◆ Lift the rolled-out pastillage to the drying board by sliding a piece of paper under it. Cut out the shape on the drying board, then remove the surplus paste.

Blisters or air pockets appear on surface of the paste

◆ These are due to excessive kneading.
◆ Burst air bubbles with a sharp needle, inserted at a 45° angle into the paste. Polish the surface with a cake smoother.

Pastillage crumbles easily and appears short

◆ Too much liquid added and more icing (confectioners') sugar kneaded in to compensate, weakening the paste by reducing the proportion of hardening agent. Knead in about 2.5ml (½ teaspoon) gum tragacanth or carboxymethyl cellulose, then check the paste.

Streaky colour and colour specks

◆ The colouring was added directly to the bulk of the paste. Always work colour into a small piece of pastillage first, then knead pieces of the strongly coloured paste into the bulk of the pastillage.
◆ Ensure that the colouring used does not have dry specks. Paste and liquid food colourings are the best.
◆ If using powder colours, dissolve them in a little water or clear alcohol before adding to the paste.

Small hollows appear on surface of rolled-out pastillage

◆ Ensure that any small pieces of dry pastillage are removed from the rolling pin and surface after cutting each piece, as they can become trapped under the pastillage giving an uneven surface when dry.

Solid shapes crack when dry

◆ Solid items will crack when dry as the paste is too thick and the moisture in the paste takes longer to evaporate. As the centre of the paste warms, it expands and the surface cracks.

Pastillage is not flat when dry

◆ Pastillage rolled too thickly.
◆ Not turned regularly during drying.
◆ Use a plywood drying board or piece of foam sponge to allow the air to circulate and dry the pastillage more quickly and evenly.

Pastillage fractures and breaks when dry

◆ To join broken pieces, either make a paste with pastillage and a little sugar glue or use soft royal icing in the same colour as the broken piece. Allow the broken piece to dry fully before use.

Applying Finishes to Pastillage

Many decorative finishes can be applied to pastillage as the surface is smooth and absorbent. Care must be taken when handling the dry pieces as they are brittle and break easily if pressure is applied, for example when removing any rough edges or tracing a design onto the surface. Place the pastillage on a piece of absorbent kitchen paper and support it on a small cake board or drying board. This will provide useful support while tracing designs and painting details onto the pastillage.

Painting and Colouring

When colouring a large area, use a large paint brush and brush smoothly back and forth. Try not to scrub the surface as this will dissolve the sugar. Avoid using watery colour on the surface which will weaken the pastillage in addition to dissolving the sugar surface.

For small areas, dilute the food colouring with water or clear alcohol. The latter evaporates quickly and is more successful when painting fine detail as there is less chance of the colour bleeding into the surrounding paste.

Gradually build up the picture, working on the background colour first, then allow this to dry before adding detail. Fine details should be added last, when all the other painting is dry. Painting techniques are illustrated in Country Scene, page 56, and Anna, page 60.

Food colourings can be mixed with white powder food colouring or whitener, water or clear alcohol to give a creamy paste consistency. This will not soak into the pastillage as quickly as liquid does and is ideal for shading and adding very fine details.

Airbrushing

An artist's airbrush (also available from cake decorating suppliers) can be used effectively for colouring pastillage, using either a mask or a stencil, or for graduating colour, creating highlights, depth and contrast on models.

Avoid holding the airbrush too close to the surface you are spraying. Secure small items to a piece of card with double-sided adhesive tape before spraying.

Sponging

A piece of natural sponge can be used to apply diluted food colouring to the pastillage. Again, water or clear alcohol can be used to dilute the food colouring. Dab the sponge gently on a test piece of pastillage before sponging the model. Try to dab the colour in a random pattern.

To apply texture and colour, mix the colour with soft royal icing and sponge this onto the pastillage.

Stippling

A short-bristled, preferably chisel-shaped, brush is used to stipple colour. Hold the brush at a 90° angle to the surface and spring it gently up and down in a random pattern. It is advisable to practise the technique on a sample piece of pastillage before colouring the model.

Powder Food Colouring

Powder food colouring is useful for highlighting and shading. Powders are concentrated and need to be mixed with cornflour (cornstarch) before use. Use a soft brush of the correct size: medium to large for larger areas; smaller for compact sections. A piece of fine foam sponge, such as cosmetic sponge, is useful for applying shading to faces. Place the model on a piece of absorbent kitchen paper and keep it away from other pieces of work as the powder food colouring tends to lightly dust surrounding areas.

Storing, Transporting and Displaying Pastillage Models

Storing

Moisture and humidity are the enemies of sugar models as they absorb moisture from the atmosphere, often with disastrous results. Small items can be stored in a cardboard box, supported on crumpled tissue paper which helps to keep them dry. Silica gel crystals absorb moisture in the atmosphere, so it is a good idea to place a small perforated bag of these in the box with the sugar model.

Transporting

A box which will protect the item is essential. Small pieces of foam sponge or crumpled tissue paper should be packed around the model. For larger items, blow into small polythene bags and position them around the base and sides of the item to act as air cushions. The drying frame shown on page 45 is the best support for figures; place the figure in the frame in a cardboard box.

Displaying

A clear glass or perspex container will protect a model from moisture, dust and damage. Keep the pastillage away from strong sunlight which will fade the food colourings.

Colouring Marzipan (Almond Paste)

There are many different food colourings available in liquid, paste and powder form. All ranges of food colouring have to conform to the regulations in the country of sale, with different types of colourings permitted according to the country.

Paste and liquid colours are best for marzipan provided that the liquid colour is strong. If a weak liquid colour is used, the amount needed to give the required strength of colour will make the marzipan sticky. The powder forms of colour are not suitable as they have to be dissolved before adding to the marzipan and sometimes small specs of undissolved colour remain to spoil the result. It is also worth noting that flavouring can be added to marzipan.

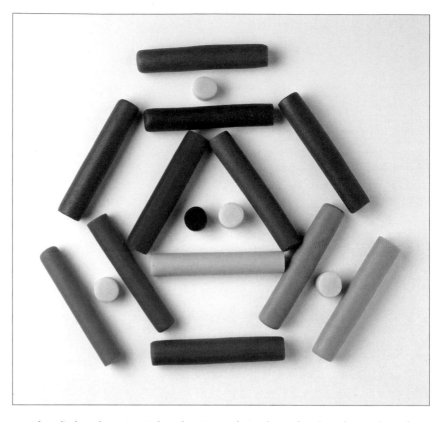

▲ *The cylinders of marzipan (almond paste) touch to indicate the colour they produce when combined. For example, yellow and blue make green, and add white to make pale green; or purple and orange make dark brown.*

Kneading in Food Colouring

First ensure that the marzipan (almond paste) is pliable and free from cracks. Break off a small piece and knead the food colouring into it so that the colour is stronger than that required for the complete portion of paste. Then work this small piece into the remaining paste, kneading the marzipan on the work surface rather than between your hands. If you colour the paste in your hands, your skin will take up the colour and the paste will become oily from being overworked.

Combining Colours

You do not have to own a vast range of food colouring: the photograph shows the variety obtained by blending pastes coloured with the three primary colours of red, yellow and blue. Use strong, dark paste colours for good results.

Green Use two parts yellow and one part blue.
Orange Use two parts yellow and one part red.
Purple Use two parts blue and one part red
The above secondary colours can be combined as follows.
Coffee Use one part orange with one part green. A little red can be added to give a more rustic or 'earthy' colour.
Dark Brown Use one part orange with one part purple.
Olive Green Use one part green with one part purple.

To lighten colours, add an equal amount of white marzipan (almond paste) or vary the proportion of white to coloured marzipan for different tints of the same colour.

To darken colours, add more of the base colour. Do not use black as it kills the other colours when combined with the marzipan. Black should only be used on its own, never when combining pastes to achieve different colours.

Try blending small pieces of different colours to develop a wider range. Use small pieces of marzipan when experimenting with colour blending before mixing larger amounts – remember to make a note of any particularly successful blends, including the proportions in which you combined the pastes.

Mixing and Storing Colours for Projects

It is best to mix all the colours and in the quantities required before you start modelling. Store the marzipan (almond paste) in plastic bags in an airtight container. The coloured marzipan will keep for 2 – 3 months but will eventually turn sour and become mouldy if forgotten in the container for longer periods.

Hints on Modelling with Marzipan

◆ Keep the model simple and neat for your first attempts and try to use a variety of modelling skills and techniques.

◆ Roll out the marzipan (almond paste) between two sheets of polythene - this way the paste can be rolled out thinly without using any icing (confectioners') sugar. The surface of the paste will also shine, which is important for the finished item.

◆ If you do get any icing sugar onto the surface, pass the modelled paste through the steam of a boiling kettle, taking care not to burn yourself. Steaming re-vitalizes the colour and gives the marzipan a fresh appearance.

◆ Take care not to steam models for too long as they will soften and sag. This is particularly true of fine items and complicated models prepared for competitions – when all the pieces have been prepared in stages over a period of time, they will need steaming for the final assembly of the model. Take great care not to make them too moist and sticky.

Glazing

An edible glaze can be used on small models which are to be used as cake top decorations. Use a spray-on glaze to keep the mar-zipan soft and give it a sheen. For competition work, it is important that the surface of the marzipan is shown without a glaze. This should be free from cracks, it should look and all joints should be neat. Avoid using too much egg white or sugar glue when securing parts of a model as they dry to a shine on the surface of the marzipan.

Painting on Marzipan

Marzipan (almond paste) can be painted provided that the surface

is smooth and free from cracks. Avoid painted areas which are deeply indented as the food colouring will bleed into any tiny cracks and spoil the finished item. It is best to allow the marzipan to set for 24 hours before painting.

For competition work you should avoid painting, adding small details by using minute pieces of marzipan. An airbrush is ideal for shading and creating life-like shadows; and the colour also dries quickly.

Problems with Marzipan

Marzipan is sticky
◆ Add more icing sugar.
◆ Ensure hands are clean and not too hot.

Marzipan becomes oily and crumbly
◆ The paste is overworked. Knead in an equal weight of fresh marzipan.

Marzipan falls back after modelling
◆ Conditions too warm. Cool your hands by rinsing under cold water.
◆ Add more icing sugar.

Marzipan becomes dry
◆ Stored for too long.
◆ Crust has formed and paste not suitable for modelling. Set aside for another use, for example in baking.

Marzipan loses shine
◆ Pass items quickly through the steam of a boiling kettle.

Marzipan will not hold shape
◆ Knead in 5ml (1 teaspoon) gum tragacanth, then shape immediately.

Rough edges to cut marzipan
◆ Use a clean plastic marzipan knife or dampen the blades of scissors when cutting.

Joints on figures and animals will not stick together
◆ Make a paste of the softened marzipan mixed with a little sugar glue. Apply to the section to be joined then support until set.

Marzipan breaks when dry
◆ As above

Marzipan smells yeasty/sour
◆ Stored incorrectly and/or for too long resulting in fermentation. Do not use the paste; discard it before further fermentation occurs.

Sugary surface and rough pieces appear
◆ Texturing or marking on the paste surface was made in the wrong direction. Work towards yourself when using modelling tools.

Specks of colour appear in marzipan
◆ Colour not blended into a small piece of paste before being added to bulk of marzipan.

Oil content of marzipan separates
◆ The use of whitening powders causes the oils in the marzipan to curdle and separate giving a rough texture and dry dull finish.
◆ To obtain a whiter marzipan, incorporate more icing sugar and liquid glucose (clear corn syrup).

Models collapse
◆ Use spaghetti for additional support, threading it through sections of the model. Allow the base to set before adding further details.
◆ Gum tragacanth can also be added to the marzipan for greater support. See above.

SKILLS AND TECHNIQUES

Preparing the Cake

The basic preparation of a cake is important for good results.

◆ The base cake should have a texture that will cut cleanly without crumbling if you are planning on cutting it into shapes. Rich fruit cake or Madeira cake are best.

Covering with Marzipan

Fill any small holes in the cake surface with marzipan. Turn the cake upside down to give a smooth, even top. Brush the cake with apricot glaze, then cover with a sheet of evenly rolled marzipan and smooth it over the cake, rounding the top edge neatly. The same method is used for a square cake, with the marzipan smoothed gently over the corners.

Apricot Glaze To make apricot glaze, heat and sieve apricot jam to remove pieces of fruit, then boil again.

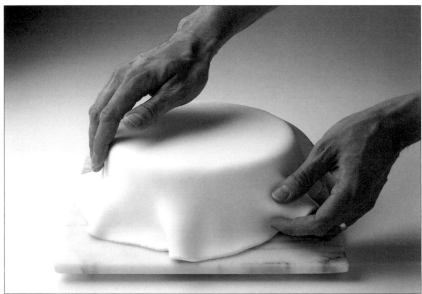

Covering with Sugarpaste

Roll out the sugarpaste to an even thickness, then brush the marzipan with clear alcohol (vodka or gin) before lifting the sugarpaste over the cake. Once the cake is loosely covered, lift the sugarpaste away from the bottom edge and smooth out folds without stretching or tearing the paste. On oddly shaped cakes ensure that you smooth the paste into curves and around corners, easing out any air bubbles or pockets from under the paste. Avoid working in a draught as this will cause the sugarpaste to form a skin quickly.

Trim the sugarpaste carefully around the edge of the cake and smooth it with your hand, then use smoothers for a perfect finish. A small pad of sugarpaste can be used to polish the surface in difficult areas on unusual-shaped cakes but ensure that there is no icing (confectioners') sugar on the paste as it will give a rough finish.

Coating a Cake with Royal Icing

When a top coat of royal icing is to be used, the marzipan (almond paste) is applied to the top and side of the cake separately, and smoothed on to make a neat, sharp corner around the top edge and on the corners of a square cake. Leave the marzipan to dry for at least 3 days before applying royal icing.

Apply at least three coats of royal icing to achieve a smooth finish, using a softer consistency of icing for a fine finish on the final coat. The top and side of a round cake are iced separately and opposite sides on an angular cake are coated separately. Paddle the icing, working it from side to side, with a palette knife on a board to reduce air bubbles before applying it to the cake. Allow each iced section to dry before coating an adjacent area.

Cake Side

Using a palette knife and a paddling action, work the icing around the side of the cake. Hold a side scraper at an angle of 45°, then rotate the cake away from you on a turntable and pull the scraper towards you.

Cake Top

Paddle soft icing over the surface to cover it completely, then hold a straight edge at an angle of 45° and pull it towards you smoothly and evenly. Lift the straight edge sharply away and remove the surplus icing with a clean palette knife. Allow to dry before applying the next coat.

Modelling Techniques for Marzipan (Almond Paste)

The animals and characters in this chapter illustrate the traditional techniques of modelling with marzipan (almond paste), based on spheres, pear shapes and cylinders. By indenting the paste or making simple cuts with scissors or a marzipan cutting knife, appealing models can be quickly formed. Since they are quick to make, these animals are ideal for commercial decoration and they are very popular in France and Switzerland, particularly during festive seasons.

◆ Hygiene is important: ensure that all utensils, surfaces and surrounding areas are clean before you start.

◆ Use good-quality marzipan which has a smooth texture and holds its shape well. If the marzipan is too soft, models will not hold their shape well, so work in a little sifted icing (confectioners') sugar. The texture is particularly important for standing characters as the weight of the head can cause the marzipan body to become squashed. Modelling Marzipan, see page 9, has been used for the characters shown.

◆ The surface of the marzipan must be smooth, free of cracks and have a good sheen. Knead the marzipan well and ensure that any colours are thoroughly blended in before you start.

◆ When using metal tools, for example for forming curves in faces and marking the surface of the marzipan, wipe the blade or cutting edge with a clean damp cloth to give a smooth result.

Simple Shapes for Friendly Characters

This form of modelling simplifies the shape of the subject to create a humorous, animated character. These models provide an opportunity for exercising your imagination and exploring marzipan as a medium for modelling.

When modelling animals – or any subject – study their shape and form. The size and proportions of the body can be adjusted and prominent features emphasized to give character. The careful use of colour and achieving clean curves are important when working with these basic forms.

The marzipan should be sufficiently soft for pieces to be joined without using egg white or sugar glue but sometimes humidity and excessively warm conditions can cause the marzipan to become too soft, making some shapes difficult to join. A little melted cooking chocolate is useful for setting the joints quickly, particularly if an electric fan is used to cool and set the chocolate.

Eyes

The eyes on these models are piped in the eye socket using a no. I piping tube (tip) and soft white royal icing. Allow the icing to dry, then paint the detail with black paste food colouring. Alternatively, melted chocolate can be piped onto the royal icing when dry.

Basic Shapes

Sphere

The sphere is used for many characters, as the base to which further shaping is applied. Cut off the required amount of marzipan and roll it into a sphere using the palms of your hands, applying even pressure as you form the shape.

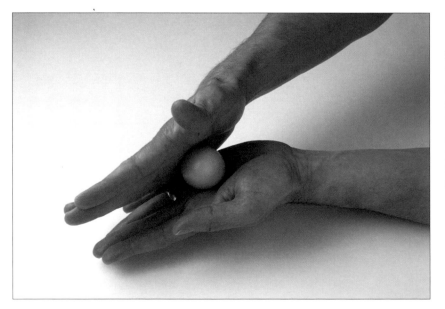

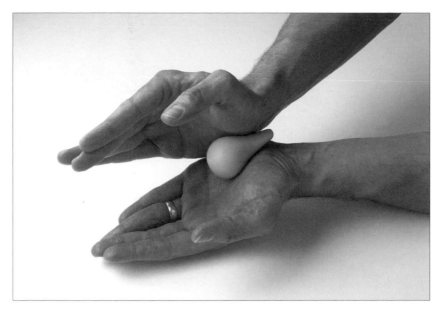

Pear

Roll a sphere, then make the crease which forms the neck of the pear by rolling the marzipan between the bases of the palms. Roll from side to side, applying pressure at one end of the sphere.

Double-ended Pear

Model a pear; the double-ended shape is then achieved by repeating the process on the wide end of the pear. The double-ended pear can be further manipulated with your fingers, for example by gently bending the elongated ends to form a head shape, as for the cat on page 18.

Cylinder

Roll the paste into a ball, then flatten it into a cylinder shape by rolling it first with your hand, then use a plastic scraper to smooth the surface and ends of the cylinder. Use a plastic marzipan knife to cut into the cylinder. Once the cylinder is cut the portions can be opened out into different positions, as for the elephant on page 24.

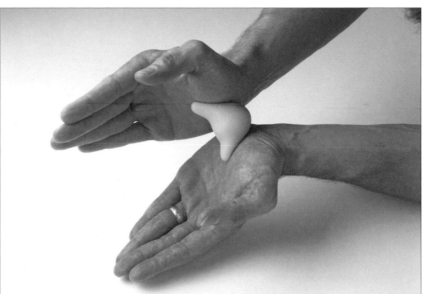

Double Cylinder

Model a cylinder, smoothing it with the scraper. Fold the cylinder in half and roll the folded end in the crease of your hand, applying pressure to form a double cylinder shape. This can be manipulated with your fingers by gently pinching the marzipan to give the desired shape. An example of this is shown on page 28, used for the clown.

Animal Characters

I have included the exact quantities of marzipan (almond paste) which I used for the main parts of each of these simple characters. You will not need to measure the smallest amounts as they can be interpreted as 'very small pieces'; even so, the weights given provide a clear indication of the proportions which should be used.

Dixie Dog
◆ Body 52g (1¾ oz)
◆ Head 15g (½ oz)
◆ Tail 5g
◆ Spots 10g

The body consists of a cylinder of white marzipan. Place the black spots on it, then roll the cylinder to blend the spots into the white marzipan. Cut the legs, making sure that the cut side of the sections are turned to face down. The hind legs are formed in the same way as the front legs but they are shorter and folded forward under the body. Model the slightly turned-up nose and cut the front of the head for the mouth. Insert the red tongue in the mouth and attach black ears. The tail is modelled from a piece of spotted paste.

Cleo Cat
◆ Body 52g (1¾ oz)
◆ Head 22g (¾ oz)
◆ Tail 3g

Colour the marzipan orange, without kneading the colour in completely to give a streaky effect. Begin by forming a pear shape for the body and a double-ended pear for the head, making the head far smaller. Pinch the ends of the double-ended pear together to form the ears. Hollow the eye sockets and ears as shown. Model a tail, two paws and a tiny black nose. Shape the mouth and attach a tiny tongue of red paste.

Lenny Lion

◆ Body 52g (1¾ oz)
◆ Head 15g (½ oz)
◆ Mane, Tail and Ears 15g (½ oz)

Form a pear shape for the body, making the thin end long enough to fold over to form the front legs. Mark the back legs and paws in the side of the wide part of the pear. Roll a sphere for the head and mark the features. Roll a cylinder for the mane, long enough to fit around the head; mark the lines once the mane is in position. Make the ears and tail, then air brush the shading on the lion using brown liquid food colouring before adding the eyes.

Ruffles Rabbit

◆ Body 45g (1½ oz)
◆ Head 15g (½ oz)
◆ Feet 5g
◆ Tail and teeth 5g

Model a pear shape for the body, making the end long enough to fold over to form the arms. Shape a smaller pear for the head and cut the slim end to form the ears. Open the ears out and mark their hollows with a dresden tool. Indent the eyes and mark the lines for the mouth. Make the feet and mark lines with a dresden tool to form the toes. Add the tail and make the teeth to complete the rabbit.

Jeremy Giraffe

◆ Body 75g (2½ oz)
◆ Markings 7g (¼ oz)

Roll out the marzipan for the markings and cut it into irregular pieces. Form a ball for the body. Then attach the markings, placing the larger pieces closer together on the top and using the smaller pieces grouped towards the base. Model a pear shape from the marked paste, keeping the bottom wider as shown. Continue to roll and shape the head and legs, marking the features. Mould the giraffe into position and support the head by placing a piece of foam sponge next to it until it has set.

Libby Lobster

◆ Body 45g (1½ oz)
◆ Claws 15g (½ oz)

Form a sphere for the body, then shape opposite ends slightly as for a pear shape. Gently bring both ends together to form the eyes and mouth. Mark the features and shape the claws as shown. Airbrush using orange food colouring, then add the eyes.

Floyd Fish

◆ Head 45g (1½ oz)
◆ Tail 30g (1 oz)
◆ Fins 7g (¼ oz)
◆ Face 5g

Roll a pear shape for the head. Gently squeeze the top part to form the back of the fish. Mark on the scales with the open end of a piping tube (tip). Mark the eyes, then add the mouth. Shape the tail and fins, and secure them to the body with sugar glue or egg white.

Air brush the fish with orange food colouring. Add the eyes and paint on the eye details.

Fishy Friends

Make two fish in contrasting colours, shaping their tails in opposite directions. Arrange the fish on a plaque of white marzipan on a larger green marzipan plaque. Position the lobster in front of the fish, giving him a small white marzipan menu to read. The trio make a novel cake top decoration or a memento for a special birthday.

Percy Penguin

- ◆ Body, black 75g (2½ oz)
- ◆ Chest, white 7g (¼ oz)
- ◆ Feet and beak 5g

Model a pear shape of black marzipan, then indent the chest. Place soft white marzipan in the chest and roll the pear. Mark the eyes and cut the flippers. Model a rounded hollow in a large piece of marzipan, then cover it with cling film (plastic wrap). Support the base of the penguin in the hollowed marzipan. Make the feet and beak, and attach with egg white or sugar glue. Air brush the chest with golden yellow liquid food colouring. Paint on the eyes.

Henry Hippo

- ◆ Body 67g (2¼ oz)
- ◆ Head 45g (1½ oz)
- ◆ Legs 37g (1¼ oz)
- ◆ Eyes, ears, feet and soles 10g

Roll a pear shape for the body, then lift the end so that it curves upwards to support the head. Shape the head and mark the mouth with the edge of a palette knife. Roll small spheres for eyes, indent them, then push onto the head. Roll a cylinder for legs and cut it into four. Shape the legs into cones and attach the soles at their wide ends. Mark the toes. Secure the legs and the head with sugar glue or egg white.

Sarah Swan

- ◆ Body 45g (1½ oz)

Roll the marzipan into a pear shape. Extend the length of the neck by rolling between the crease of both hands. Curl the top part of the neck around and support it with a small piece of foam sponge, if necessary, until set. Add a beak of black and orange, and paint on the eyes when set.

Swan Plaques

These swans, displayed on poured-sugar plaques are the ideal decorations for a single-tier wedding, engagement or other special celebration cake.
Model some marzipan rushes, see page 39, and make a water lily flower using a small daisy cutter.
When the marzipan is set, the rushes can be secured to the sugar plaque with a little of the cooked sugar.

Boiled Sugar Plaques

Place 250g (8 oz/1 cup) sugar in a heavy-bottomed saucepan and add 90ml (3 fl oz/⅓ cup) water. Stir in 5ml (1 teaspoon) liquid glucose (clear corn syrup). Heat, stirring gently occasionally, until the sugar has dissolved. Stop stirring and bring the syrup to the boil. Cook until the syrup registers 152°C (310°F) on a sugar (candy) thermometer. *Do not stir the syrup at all once the sugar has dissolved and it begins to boil.* Lay a small crumpled sheet of foil on a piece of marble or thick heatproof chopping board. Place a lightly oiled metal pastry (cookie) cutter on the foil. Carefully pour the cooked sugar over the foil in the cutter. To create a marble blue plaque, drop two or three drops of liquid blue food colouring into the syrup just as it is about to reach the required temperature and gently swirl the pan to part mix the colour.

Take care when pouring hot syrup. Leave the plaque to set and partly cool before removing the cutter – remember that the cutter may still be very hot so protect your hand with a cloth. When cool, cut around the poured sugar plaque leaving a clean edge. Secure the rushes to the plaque by dipping them into a little of the leftover cooked syrup, reheating it slightly until melted if it has set in the saucepan. Do not stir the syrup or the sugar will crystallize.

Opposite: A selection of ideas for displaying the animals on plaques that are ideal for decorating simple cakes.

Ellie Elephant

- ◆ *Body 60g (2 oz)*
- ◆ *Head 30g (1 oz)*
- ◆ *Ears 10g*
- ◆ *Tusks 3g*

Shape a 10cm (4 in) long cylinder and make 3cm (1½ in) cuts into both ends. Shape the cut edges, then open the front feet and bring the rear feet forward. Mark the soles of the feet. Pinch the lower back and make a small snip for the tail. Make an elongated pear shape for the head. Mark the eyes, mouth and small holes for tusks. Halve the marzipan for the ears and shape them. Press the soft ears onto the head. Add tusks and eyes.

Dandy Deer

- ◆ *Body 60g (2 oz)*
- ◆ *Head 15g (½ oz)*
- ◆ *Neck 3g*
- ◆ *Antlers 5g*
- ◆ *Ears, mouth and feet 5g*

Model a pear shape for the body, then flatten it on both sides. Cut the legs and stand the body upright. Make a small snip into the marzipan for the tail. Shape the head and mark the eyes. Place the mouth in position and cut it with the edge of a small round cutter. Roll the marzipan for the antlers, then use a plastic marzipan knife to cut the ends and separate the pieces slightly. Roll a small flattened sphere for the neck. Attach the nose and antlers, then secure the head to the body with sugar glue or melted chocolate. Support the head with a piece of foam sponge until set.

Simple Figures

These animated marzipan (almond paste) figures are made using the basic modelling techniques shown on the previous pages. Although their construction is extremely simple, the features have been emphasized to give the models character. You can make many different characters using this technique. Once you have mastered the basic skills, your imagination can take over.

Whatever your theme, these shapes can be adapted to provide a fun range of models; for example, the basic form for the standing clown can be used as a base for a fisherman, with suitable clothing and features added.

Rolling Out Marzipan Between Polythene

When rolling out small amounts of marzipan (almond paste), for example to make clothes for modelled characters, placing the paste between two sheets of polythene prevents it from sticking to the board, making it easier to handle. This method also gives the marzipan a good shine.

▼ *Rolling out marzipan between polythene*

Father Christmas (Santa Claus)

◆ *Legs 45g (1½ oz)*
◆ *Body 22g (¾ oz)*
◆ *Head 15g (½ oz)*
◆ *Arms 5g*
◆ *Sleeves 7g (¼ oz)*
◆ *Nose and mouth 5g*
◆ *Moustache and beard 7g (¼ oz)*
◆ *Boots and buckle 15g (½ oz)*

Roll a cylinder about 10cm (4 in) long for the legs, then fold it in half. Squash the paste down gently to shape the legs. Make a small indent into the top of the legs to form a hollow in which to place the body. Shape a sphere for the body, then place it in the hollow. Shape a

> **MODELLING MEMO**
>
> *When modelling standing figures, work a little additional icing (confectioners') sugar into the marzipan to make a firmer paste.*

sphere for the head and mark the eyes, taking care not to mark them too far apart. Shape the mouth and nose, and attach them to the head. Mark the curve for the mouth with the wide end of a piping tube (tip).

Shape the boots then position the legs on them. Roll a small cylinder and cut it in half for arms. Shape the hand and mark the fingers without cutting through the marzipan. Roll out two 3cm (1¼ in) squares for sleeves and wrap them around the arms. Add a small square for the belt buckle. Position the arms on the body, then attach the head. Cut out the beard and moustache using 5cm (2 in) and 3.5cm (1½ in) round cutters. Attach these around the mouth and under the nose.

Cut out a 10.5 x 4cm (4¼ x 1¾ in) rectangle of rolled-out marzipan for the hat. Bring the top two corners together to form a cone shape. Cut the small triangle shape off, then open out the cone and re-form it over the head. Cut out and attach a thin band of

marzipan for the hat edge. Pipe the eyes with white royal icing. When the icing is dry, paint on the pupils. Pipe short lines for the eyebrows and a small bulb on the end of the hat. The cheeks and nose are coloured with diluted liquid food colouring.

Snowman

- ◆ Body 45g (1½ oz)
- ◆ Head 15g (½ oz)
- ◆ Arms 5g each
- ◆ Scarf 15g (½ oz) each of two colours
- ◆ Hat and buttons 7g (¼ oz)

Shape a cylinder for the body and a sphere for the head. Roll small cylinders for the arms, shape them and secure to the body in the required pose. Roll out strips in two colours for the striped scarf, see page 41, then place it around the top of the body. Attach the head and add a small cone of

marzipan for the nose. Add the buttons. Shape the top of the hat and cut the base using a 2.5 cm (1 in) cutter. Place the hat on the figure and adjust the position

before painting the eyes and mouth using a fine paintbrush and paste food colouring.

Time to Go!

Father Christmas' reindeer is obviously a little concerned about the long journey ahead. The Christmas trees are made from cones of marzipan (almond paste) placed on a small, thin bottle. The cuts are made with small scissors which are dampened slightly first so that they make clean cuts in the paste. Sifted icing (confectioners') sugar adds a snowy touch. The group is arranged on a sugarpaste plaque, trimmed with fine red ribbon.

sections along the top of the jacket.

Place the arms on the jacket and fold the sleeve sections over them. Form the arms into a curved shape, then position them around the body. Add the buttons. Shape a sphere for the head and indent the eyes. Shape the mouth section and mark the smile with the wide end of a piping tube (tip). Make tiny spheres for the ears, hollow their centres and attach to the head.

Cut two small rectangles of marzipan for the hair, mark lines on them and secure to the head. Pipe the eyes with white royal icing and paint the detail with black paste food colouring when the icing is dry. Add a bow tie to complete the clown.

Sitting Clown

- Body and legs 60g (2 oz)
- Head 22g (¾ oz)
- Hair 5g
- Arms 7g (¼ oz)
- Shirt 10g
- Shoes 10g

Roll a 10cm (4 in) cylinder for the body and legs, then make a 4cm (3¾ in) cut into one end. Open out the cut to make legs, turning the cut edge face down. Cut a 4 x 3cm (3¾ x 1¼ in) rectangle of rolled-out

marzipan for the shirt, then place it on the body. Mark a line down the middle of the shirt. Shape the shoes and attach them to the legs. Roll an 11cm (4½ in) cylinder for the arms. Shape the hands and cut a small 'V' shape for the thumbs. Mark on the fingers but do not cut through the marzipan. Cut out a 9cm (3¾ in) rectangle of rolled-out paste for the jacket. Cut a small piece out of each side of the paste as shown to create the sleeve

Standing Clown

- Legs 45g (1½ oz)
- Body 22g (¾ oz)
- Head and mouth 15g (½ oz)
- Arms 7g (¼ oz)
- Hair 7g (¼ oz)
- Shoes 15g (½ oz)
- Jacket 30g (1 oz)

Roll a cylinder about 9cm (3½ in) long for the legs. Fold the marzipan in half, then shape the legs further by rolling them between the curve of both hands. Make a small hollow on the top for the body. Shape a cone for the body and mark a line down the middle. Place the cone in the hollow on the legs. Shape the shoes and place the legs on them. Add strips of paste for braces. Cut out the jacket, trimming the corners and making 'V' snips as shown. Place the jacket on the body without folding back the lapels.

Roll a 9.5cm (3¾ in) cylinder for the arms. Mark a line at each end for hands with four

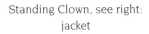

Standing Clown, see right: jacket

Sitting Clown, see above: jacket

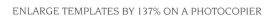

ENLARGE TEMPLATES BY 137% ON A PHOTOCOPIER

lines for the fingers. Roll out two 3.5cm (1½ in) squares and wrap around the ends of the arms for sleeves. Shape the arms around the body, securing them at shoulder height. Fold back the lapels. Add the buttons.

Shape a sphere for the head and mark on tear-drop shaped eyes. Shape the mouth and secure to the head, marking the smile with the wide end of a piping tube (tip). Add the nose. For hair, push the marzipan through a fine sieve or use a clay gun modelling tool. Pipe the eyes with white royal icing and paint the detail with black paste food colouring when the icing is dry. Add a small bow tie.

Clowning Around

This jolly pair make a fun centrepiece for a child's birthday cake. Arrange the pair of clowns on a marzipan plaque, adding small coloured circles and a marzipan number to represent the age of the child. Vary the characters and colours as you wish.

Animal Caricatures

This particular style of detailed modelling is suitable for exhibition work, for special commissions or other specific projects. All the heads for these characters are modelled separately from the body, then allowed to dry in an airtight container for 12 hours. This gives the marzipan (almond paste) time to set, the surface becomes firmer and does not mark as easily but the paste does not form a crust. The heads can still be joined to the bodies and the edges of the fresh marzipan can be blended onto them.

An indented sphere of marzipan, enclosed in a polythene bag, provides support for the head while the marzipan is soft, allowing fine detail to be modelled without squashing or distorting the shape of the head. Supporting the head in this way also leaves both hands free for modelling.

I use a pair of dresden tools, one in each hand, for modelling teeth and eyes, giving access to tiny areas which fingers are too large to reach. The recipe for the marzipan is given on page 9 – the addition of liquid glucose (clear corn syrup) and icing (confectioners') sugar provides the required texture and durability.

Size and Proportion

Each of the characters measures 7.5 – 8.5cm (3 – 3½ in) in height. The amount of marzipan for each is given as a weight for the head and the body. It is not practical to weigh the tiny portions used for the details. The comparative sizes of the smaller pieces is clearly shown by the stages of modelling set out in the photographs. The body takes one and a half times the quantity of marzipan used for the head. If you find that the proportions of the head need adjusting for your model, small pieces of marzipan can be moulded onto the base of the head in the early stages of forming the character.

▼ *Texturing the marzipan to resemble the animal's coat*

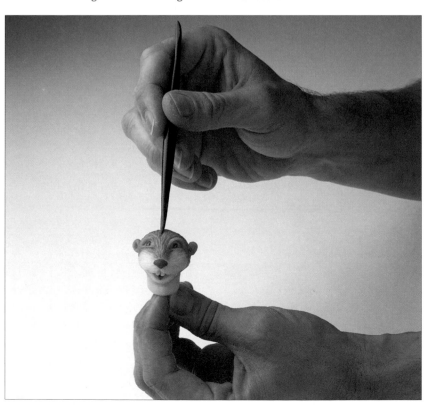

Method of Modelling the Heads and Necks

The basic shape of each head is formed from either a sphere or pear shape, which has a hole made underneath using a cone tool. For the neck, a smaller piece of paste is rolled into a cylinder and a cocktail stick (toothpick) with the point cut off one end is inserted into the cylinder. The blunted end of the cocktail stick is pushed into the head and secured by blending the edges of the marzipan together to conceal the join.

The character is then created following the stages illustrated. When the modelling on the head is complete, the cocktail stick protruding from the neck is inserted in a piece of styrofoam such that the neck rests on the foam to prevent the cocktail stick from pushing through the top of the head. The model is then placed in an airtight container to set for 12 hours before being attached to the body.

Hats

Information on making and applying hats is given on pages 130 and 135.

Applying Facial Detail

It is the detail which is applied when modelling which brings the individual characters to life. The following standard techniques are used for all the characters.

Texture
Hold the head by the cocktail stick (toothpick) and use the pointed end of a dresden tool to mark the texture in a forward direction. Follow the contours of the animal's head, applying the texture so that it flows around the eyes and down the back of the head.

Mouth

Apart from the pose of the body, the mouth and eyes make key contributions to expression. Use the wider end of a dresden tool to hollow out the inside of the mouth and to form the creases in the corners of the mouth. Smooth the surface of the paste after any indents are made to retain the shine.

Teeth

Two different techniques may be used. The first is to roll very small pieces of white marzipan into pointed cone shapes, then cut short lengths for the size of the teeth and insert them into the mouth with a dresden tool.

The second technique is to shape a small square of white marzipan for the two front teeth and insert it into the top of the mouth. Make a small cut or mark into the marzipan to separate the teeth or indicate that there are two teeth. This technique is shown on the rabbit on page 31.

Eyes

Fill the eye sockets with white marzipan, ensuring that you have pushed the marzipan in deeply otherwise it will give a staring or bulging impression. Shape a small semi-circle of marzipan on the white of the eye, then apply a smaller semi-circle of black. A very small speck of white marzipan can be added to the black to add a glint to the expression. The colours of the eyes can be varied and two different colours can be used for the first semi-circle before adding the black. This is useful for younger-looking characters.

Creating Individual Caricatures

◆ Follow the basic method of modelling the heads and necks for each of the characters, using the first two stages set out in the relevant photograph as a guide to modelling a sphere or a pear shape. Then continue to build up the individual characteristics as described and illustrated.

Rabbit

◆ Body 45g (1½ oz)
◆ Head 30g (1 oz)

Mark the eyes with the ball tool. Mark the nose and mouth with a small palette knife or marzipan knife. Roll pieces of marzipan into shape for the ears. Roll a small piece of pink marzipan for the inside of each ear, pinching the edges of the paste to make them thinner. Secure the ears to the head, blending the join with a dresden tool. Roll two tear-drop shapes from white marzipan and push them into the eye sockets with a dresden tool. Model the open mouth and insert the dresden tool, then gently push the cheeks out from the inside to give the shape of the face. Press a thin piece of pink marzipan into the lower part of the mouth. Follow the stages on page 30 for eyes and teeth. Place the head in an airtight container for 12 hours, then complete the character as shown on page 34.

Fox

◆ Body 45g (1½ oz)
◆ Head 30g (1 oz)

Place a small piece of white marzipan on the upper jaw section, then blend the paste into the brown marzipan. Form the lower jaw from white marzipan, shaping it into a hollowed cylinder. Attach this to base of the upper jaw and blend the edges of the paste together. Roll small pieces of brown marzipan for the ears and blend small pieces of white marzipan on top, then shape the ears. Position the base of the ears on the head just below the eye line, smoothing the edges to ensure a good join. Mould a small piece of pink paste into the top and lower jaw and mark the roof of the mouth with a dresden tool. Make the eyes and teeth as shown on page 30. The eyebrows are formed by rolling small pieces of darker-coloured marzipan into thin strips, then applying them over the eye lids. Place the head in an airtight container for 12 hours, then complete the character as shown on page 34.

Hedgehog

◆ Body 32g (1⅛ oz)
◆ Head 22g (¾ oz)

The prickles are shown in the photograph for the purposes of explaining the way in which the head is created but they can be easily broken if they are added in the first stages of modelling. It is

better to add the prickles when the figure is completed and dressed.

The head and neck are modelled in one piece, between the fingers, then modelled onto the cut-off cocktail stick (toothpick). Mark the eyes with a dog bone tool, then shape with the dresden tool. Cut the mouth with the edge of a thin palette knife. Hollow out the mouth and mark a line from the mouth to the end of the nose. Make the eyes as shown on page 30. Make two small ears and attach them just below eye level. Form the tongue and texture the marzipan as shown on page 29.

The prickles are made from small pieces of marzipan, rolled into thin-ended cone shapes. They are attached to the head in rows, alternating the position for each row so that prickles in successive rows sit in front of spaces in previous rows. Place the head in an airtight container for 12 hours,

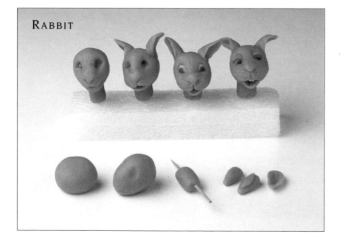

RABBIT

FOX

HEDGEHOG

BADGER

then complete the character as shown on page 34.

Badger

◆ Body 45 g (1½ oz)
◆ Head 30g (1 oz)

Colour the black and white marzipan, then ensure that your hands are free from any colouring before you start to model the animal. Shape the head into a longer pear shape, tapering the snout. Roll two small black cylinders of marzipan. Taper each of these at one end, then place on the head, leaving a band of white marzipan showing down the middle. Shape the eyes with a dresden tool. Cut the mouth with the edge of a thin palette knife. Open the lower jaw and hollow it slightly with a dog bone tool. Mould pink marzipan into the lower jaw.

Shape white marzipan into the eye sockets, smoothing it with a dresden tool. Mould the ears from small spheres of white marzipan, with small pieces of black

The Caravan Park cake from River-bank Revelry, see page 126.

FROG

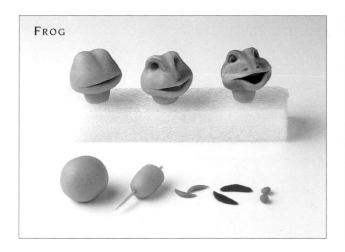

MOUSE

marzipan placed on top. Cup the ears slightly with the dresden tool, then attach them to the head. The ears are placed towards the back of the head, slightly above the eye line. Texture the surface of the marzipan, then add the eye details as shown on page 30. Place the head in an airtight container for 12 hours, then complete the character as shown on page 34.

Frog
◆ Body 45g (1½ oz)
◆ Head 30g (1 oz)

The head and neck are modelled in one piece. At the next stage, the body is formed directly under the chin, so the neck is shortened. The different colours of green on the head are achieved by using darker pieces of marzipan shaped into small spheres, flattened, then applied to the head and smoothed down with the flat end of a dresden tool. Manipulate the head into shape with your fingers and a dog bone tool.

Shape the eyes with a dresden tool and cut the mouth with a thin palette knife. Hollow out the lower part of the mouth and blend in darker green marzipan on the head. Roll a small piece of darker green marzipan and shape it over the eye sockets. Make indents over the eyes. Fill the mouth opening with red marzipan, smoothing it down to shape the mouth. Form the eyes from yellow-orange marzipan, then place them in the

eye sockets. Place pieces of black marzipan on the eyes for pupils and add small semi-circles of white marzipan. Mark around the mouth with a dresden tool.

The surface of the frog is left smooth, so try to avoid leaving finger prints in the paste. Place the head in an airtight container for 12 hours, then complete the character as shown on page 34.

Mouse
◆ Body 32g (1⅛ oz)
◆ Head 22g (¾ oz)

Lift the end of the nose gently, then mark the eyes with a dresden tool. Make a small cut for the mouth with the thin edge of a palette knife, then shape the lower part. Place a small piece of marzipan into the lower part of the mouth and smooth it into shape. Use the veining end of the dresden tool to mark a line for the snout from the base of the mouth to the end of the nose. Make the eyes, see page 30: to make the younger character shown, place a small piece of light brown marzipan over the white, then add a small piece of black on top.

Mould the ears from small pieces of marzipan, adding an inner, slightly smaller, pink ear to each. Blend the edges of the marzipan between two pieces of polythene, then attach the ears to the head, smoothing and blending the join. The teeth are made from white marzipan, shaped in a small

rectangle. Mark the middle of the pair of teeth, then use the dresden tool to insert them in the mouth, pushing the top of the teeth into the roof of the mouth so that just the ends of the teeth show. Add a small nose. Texture the paste lightly with the dresden tool, using only gentle pressure for the younger character shown. Place the head in an airtight container for 12 hours, then complete the character as shown on page 34.

Weasel
◆ Body 52g (1¾ oz)
◆ Head 32g (1⅛ oz)

Leave 3g (⅛ oz) of the marzipan light brown, then colour the remainder light grey; reserve a small piece for the ears. Shape the grey head and neck, making the neck longer for ease of handling. Mark the eye sockets. Save a small piece of the brown marzipan for the ears; then roll the remainder into a small ball and flatten it. Place this below the nose. Blend the grey and brown marzipan to form the cheeks.

Cut the mouth with the edge of a thin palette knife and shape it with a dresden tool. Form the eyes, see page 30, then roll small pieces of grey marzipan and shape them over the top to form the eye lids.

Fill the lower part of the mouth with pink marzipan and make two small white teeth, shaped into a small square and marked in half

WEASEL

STOAT

with a knife. Insert the teeth in the front of the upper jaw. Shape a red tongue and insert it in the mouth. Texture the head and make two small ears by cupping small pieces of grey marzipan with a ball tool. Place brown marzipan in the ears and apply a little pressure with the ball tool to shape them. Secure to the head. Place the head in an airtight container for 12 hours, then complete the character as shown on page 34.

Stoat
◆ Head and body 45g (1½oz)
◆ Head 30g (1 oz)

Colour a quarter of the marzipan light brown and reserve small pieces for ears. Form the neck from the white marzipan. Shape the head from the remaining white and brown marzipan rolled together.

Mark the eye sockets, then cut the mouth with the edge of a thin palette knife. Fill the lower part of the mouth with a small piece of pink marzipan and form the teeth from white marzipan, cutting it down the middle to form two teeth. Insert the teeth in the top of the mouth with a dresden tool. Shape a small red tongue. Shape the eyes. Make two small ears from brown marzipan, cup them with the ball tool, then join them securely to the head. Texture the surface with a dresden tool. Place the head in an airtight container for 12 hours, then complete the character as shown on page 34.

Completing the Animal Caricatures

The following skills for modelling the body and creating clothes are used to complete all the animal caricatures shown in The Happy Couple, see page 38, Happy New Year, see page 53, and River-bank Revelry, see page 126, projects. Marzipan (almond paste) is used in each case. These techniques can be used as a basic guide for creating a variety of different characters by adapting the colours and clothing to suit the project.

Modelling a Body

The basic method is used for all the animals but the marzipan can be modelled slightly differently in some cases. For example, the mouse bride has a waist and a bust.

Torso
Take a piece of marzipan about one and a half times the size of the head and shape it into a cylinder. Make a hole at one end of the cylinder large enough to accommodate the neck. Remove the cocktail stick from the modelled head and insert the neck into the cylinder. Smooth the edges of the paste around the neck to neaten and secure the join. Shape the lower part of the body ready to join onto the legs.

▼ *Attaching the head to the torso.*

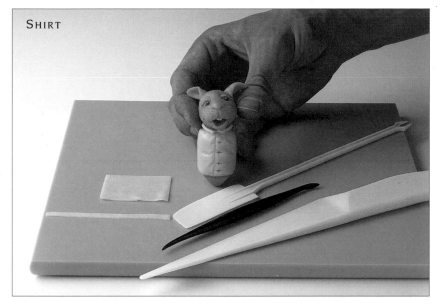

SHIRT

LEGS AND SHOES

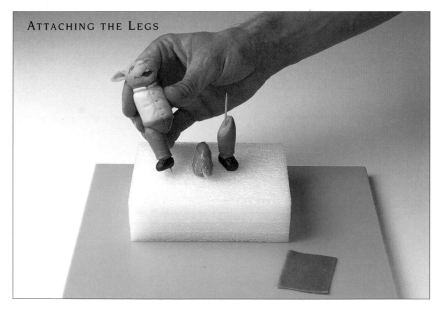

ATTACHING THE LEGS

Shirt

Roll out the marzipan between two sheets of polythene, then cut a rectangle for the shirt and place it on the body. Cut off surplus marzipan with small scissors or a plastic marzipan knife. Mark a line down the middle and mark the buttonholes. Cut a strip of marzipan long enough to go around the neck to form the collar.

Legs and Shoes

Roll out the marzipan between two sheets of polythene and leave to rest for 5 minutes before cutting out the shoes. Roll a cylinder for the legs and cut two lengths about three-quarters of the length of the body for a standing character. If the character is sitting, the legs should be half the length of the body. Shape the feet. Cut a small rectangle large enough to cover one foot from the rolled-out paste. Join this around the back of the foot and trim the excess paste. Repeat for the second foot. Stand the legs on the rolled-out paste and cut around the bottom of each foot for the soles. Mark the heel and holes for laces.

Add the laces when the character is completed: roll thin strands of marzipan, shape them into a figure-of-eight and apply to the tops of the shoes.

Attaching the Legs to the Body

It is not necessary to support the legs with cocktail sticks (tooth-picks) if the character is sitting; for a standing figure, it is important to follow the instructions for supporting the legs.

Cover each leg with a piece of thinly rolled marzipan to make trousers, placing the join at the back if the character is sitting or on the inside of the leg for a standing figure. Apply a band of marzipan around the waist for the top of the trousers. Carefully insert a cocktail stick (toothpick) into each leg, from the base of each shoe. Then attach the legs to the body.

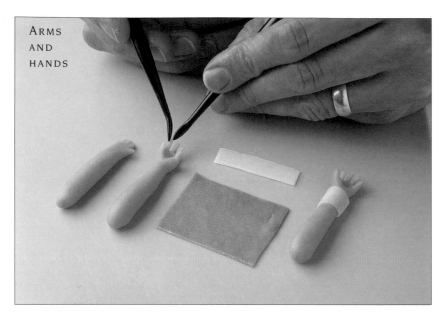

ARMS
AND
HANDS

Smooth the joins in the marzipan and mark any creases in the trousers where the legs would naturally bend. Stand the figure on styrofoam, pushing the protruding cocktail sticks into the foam. Cover a small piece of marzipan with cling film (plastic wrap) and place between the legs to help support the body weight. Cover the figure with a polythene bag and leave to set for 12 hours. Remove the cocktail sticks when the character is completed.

Modelling Arms and Hands

Roll a cylinder of marzipan about twice the length of the body, then cut it in half. Model a hand at one end of each cylinder. Cut a 'V' shape for the thumb, then make three further cuts to give four fingers. Cut a small piece of paste from between each finger. Open out the fingers and, if possible, gently soften the edges of each finger between your index finger and thumb. If you have difficulty in modelling the tiny fingers, use two dresden tools, one in each hand.

If the character is intended to hold an object, then model the fingers around a cocktail stick (toothpick) to adjust their position and form a grasp. Remove the cocktail stick and leave the marzipan to set. The object can be placed in the grasp of the figure once the model has set.

Modelling Sleeves, Waistcoat and Jacket

Place small strips of marzipan around the ends of the arms to form cuffs. Cut two rectangles of rolled-out marzipan large enough to wrap around the arms. Fold surplus paste around the top of the arm. If you want to make a tie, then cut out and apply this before making the waistcoat.

To cut the waistcoat and jacket to size, hold a piece of rolled-out marzipan around the figure, make a small mark on the paste where it will meet, then carefully remove

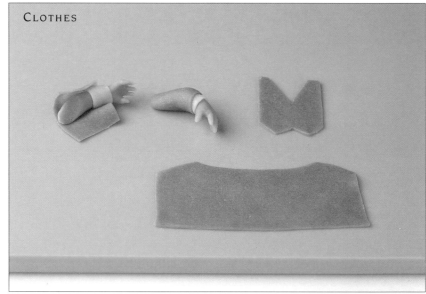

CLOTHES

and cut the paste to size using small scissors or a thin palette knife. Use this method for both garments, then apply them to the figure when they are neatly cut to shape.

Attaching the Arms to the Body

Cut the top of each arm at an angle of 45°, so that they fit snugly against the shoulders. Mark any creases in the marzipan where the arm will bend, then smooth the paste over the join.

Once the arms are attached other small features, such as pockets and buttons, may be attached to the clothing.

ATTACHING
THE ARMS

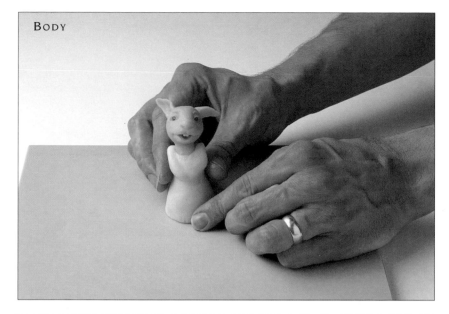

BODY

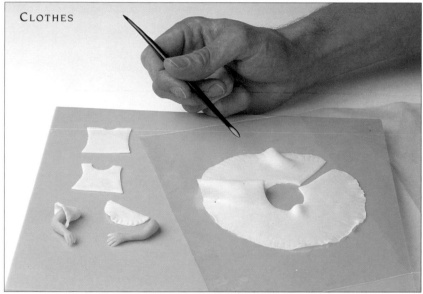

CLOTHES

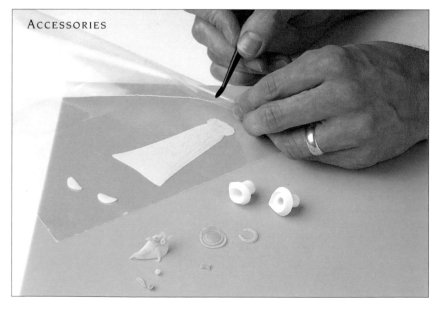

ACCESSORIES

The Bride

The skills explained here for forming the body of the bride and making her clothing are also used for other characters featured on Happy New Year, see page 53, and River-bank Revelry, see page 126. The colours and exact style of clothing can be changed to make a variety of individual characters.

The Bride's Body

Make the marzipan cylinder for the body about two and a half times the height of the head and neck. Female characters are modelled slightly shorter than males. Hollow out the top of the cylinder to take the neck. Remove the cocktail stick (toothpick), then insert the neck into the body section and smooth the join around the neck. You can insert a short piece of spaghetti into the neck for support.

Shape the body to form the waist and bust. Leave the figure to set for 12 hours, if possible, before applying the skirt.

Making The Dress

Roll out the marzipan between two sheets of polythene. Cut two small rectangles for the front and back of the bodice. Cut the neckline with the wide end of a piping tube (tip). Apply to the character, smoothing down joins. Measure the distance from the waist to the worksurface, then cut out a circle of rolled-out marzipan with a diameter of twice this distance. Cut out a small circle to fit the bride's waist from the large circle. Cut the resulting ring of paste so that it can be wrapped around the bride.

Place the paste on a sheet of polythene and smooth the edges by rubbing your fingers around them. Flute the edge by pressing it with a dresden tool before removing from the polythene. Gather the marzipan in small sections and secure it around the waist, smoothing down the join and adjusting the folds.

Make the arms as shown on page 36 but slightly smaller. For the sleeves, cut a small circle of marzipan, then cut it in half and flute the edges as for the skirt. Gather the sleeves around the arms, then join to the body, smoothing down the join.

Adding Accessories

For the collar, cut a small circle of rolled-out marzipan and cut it in half to make the two sides of the collar. Place them in position around the bride's neck and add a small bow in the middle. The head dress is cut from thinly rolled marzipan and textured between two sheets of polythene. Gather the top of the head dress and attach it to the top of the bride's head. Drape the head dress over one shoulder.

Small flowers are made as shown on page 45, with the marzipan thinned between two sheets of polythene. Cut out a petal shape of rolled-out white marzipan for the back of the bouquet and model a small handle on the back so that it can be inserted in the bride's hand. Secure all the small flowers to the base of the bouquet and the head dress as you make them.

A small horse shoe is made by cutting marzipan with two different rose petal cutters.

The Happy Couple

Arrange the bride and groom on a small cake board covered with the same coating as used on the cake and trimmed with narrow ribbon. Add small pieces of different-coloured marzipan for the confetti.

Modelling Techniques for Textures and Effects on Objects

This is an area of different skills from those explained by modelling the various characters and figures in the early part of the chapter. Many of the techniques shown here are useful for pastillage as well as for marzipan (almond paste).

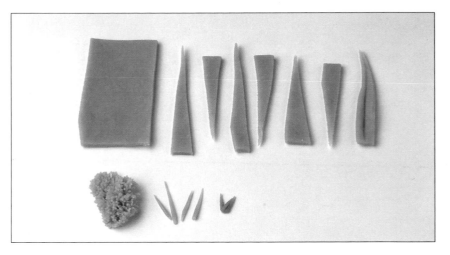

Grass and Rushes

Grass is formed by pressing marzipan through a nylon sieve or by extruding it through a clay gun modelling tool. The marzipan must be soft so that it can be pushed through the sieve or pressed through the clay gun.

Tufts of grass add variety and detail. These are made by rolling the marzipan into thin strips, then positioning two or three together on the textured base.

Grass textured effects can also be obtained by using modelling tools. Using the wide end of a dresden tool, indent the soft marzipan using a cutting action. A small ball tool can be used for a different effect by pushing it irregularly into the surface of the paste. If you are texturing a large area, ensure that you have

sufficient time to complete the effect before the surface of the marzipan sets as the result will be a rough effect.

Rushes and reeds are made by rolling the marzipan between two polythene sheets and cutting out the individual rushes using a marzipan knife or a thin-edged palette knife. Mark a line down the middle of each rush with a dresden tool and smooth the edges of the paste to ensure that they are not rough.

Stones

Take a mixture of pieces of different-coloured marzipan and knead them together without blending the colours completely,

▼ *Paving, bricks and stones.*

▲ Making grass.

to give a streaky effect. Shape small pieces of rock and texture the surface slightly with the veining end of a dresden tool. Mark lines along the rock such that they cross over each other, and make a few small holes in the paste. Take care not to make the surface of the marzipan rough by marking too deeply with the tool.

Bricks

Roll out the marzipan between two sheets of polythene. Cut pieces about 1.5cm (¾ in) long and 8mm (⅓ in) wide and smooth their edges. Roll a thin strip of marzipan, then lay the bricks on it in a interwoven pattern, laying the bricks side by side but staggered in relation to the previous row. Smooth small pieces of marzipan between each joint.

The brickwork can be built up on the surface which is to be covered or assembled on a sheet of polythene, then positioned on the model when completed.

Another way of indicating brick-work is by embossing the freshly rolled marzipan or other modelling material with a small toy building brick.

Paving

Roll out the marzipan and cut out rectangles. If you want to join the

paving with grouting in between them, then roll a thin cylinder of different-coloured marzipan. Lay the cylinder along the edges of each paving slab and cut a thin strip to make the grout. If you want to join the slabs without a grout effect, be sure to smooth the cut edges before joining them together.

Pathway

Roll out and cut the marzipan for the basic shape of the path. Blend a range of different colours together for stones. Cut the paste into different-sized pieces and flatten them between two sheets of polythene. Place the pieces on the path and smooth around each with a dresden tool. Polish the tops of the stones with a small piece of polythene.

Sand Effect

Roll out the marzipan and place it on the model. Crush a small piece of foil and dampen it slightly. Emboss the fresh marzipan with the crumpled foil but try not to make the surface of the marzipan rough.

Gravel

Roll out three or four different colours of marzipan thinly. Cut into thin strips and leave to dry, uncovered, for 30 minutes. Cut the paste into very small pieces. Prepare a coloured base of marzipan and brush it with a little sugar glue – avoid using too much which will mark the surface of the marzipan when dry. Scatter the tiny pieces of coloured paste over the base to give a gravel effect.

Water

Blend together marzipan coloured in two shades of blue, a little white and green. The pastes should be part mixed to give a

▲ *A selection of textures and effects explained on this and the previous page.*

streaky effect. Roll the paste into a cylinder, then form it into a coil. Roll out the paste swirled with colour between two sheets of polythene and select the most interesting side to be placed uppermost on the model. Using a dog bone tool, follow the swirls of colour in the paste and mark the surface. These marks can be deepened slightly with the wide

▼ *Stripes and inlay effects (opposite).*

end of the tool and ripples may be marked where a fish breaks the surface of the water, where a fishing line is cast or around a boat. This effect is shown on the River-bank Revelry cake, see page 126.

Snow

Snow is made from white marzipan with extra icing (confectioners') sugar added. Roll out the marzipan

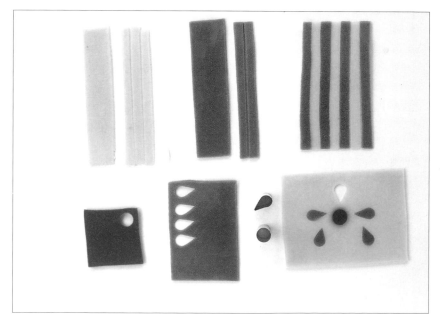

into the shape of the required area of snow. Using the widest end of the dresden tool, pull the surface of the marzipan forwards to open the texture of the paste and create a coarse texture implying a light snow covering. If the marzipan is too dry, work in a little liquid glucose (clear corn syrup).

Do not add whitening powders to marzipan as they cause the oil in the paste to curdle and the marzipan to dry out quickly.

Stripes and Inlay Effects

For both techniques, it is important to roll the different colours of marzipan to the same thickness.

For stripes, place strips of marzipan of alternate colours side by side on a sheet of plastic. Cover with a second sheet of plastic and smooth the paste to flatten and join the alternate strips of colour into stripes. The side which is facing down will be the neatest side.

If the striped paste is to be used for clothing, roll out a piece of marzipan thinly, separate from the stripes, then lay it over the top of the flattened stripes and roll the double paste again to bond the striped paste to the plain paste. This prevents the stripes from falling apart when the paste is wrapped around a figure.

Woodgrain Effect

The floorboards used on the Happy New Year project, see page 53, are made using this technique. Roll three different shades of brown marzipan together. Flatten the paste and cut it into lengths. Marks are made using the veining end of a dresden tool, following the streaks on the surface of the marzipan. Make small holes for nails and cover them with tiny pieces of grey marzipan. It is best to attach the floorboards directly on the surface which you want to cover.

▲ *Woodgrain effect.*

Pastillage Figure Modelling

Figures modelled in pastillage or modelling paste are quite different from the simple forms and characters already explained. This form of modelling is used to create life-like results.

This modelling cannot be compared to that using other sugar mediums: on its own, pastillage dries quickly allowing only limited time for shaping the paste. Therefore equal quantities of flower paste and sugarpaste are combined to make modelling paste. This is allowed to mature for 24 hours so that the strength and durability of the paste is maximized before use. Although the paste may appear dry on the surface, the sugarpaste content retains moisture and the modelling paste will soon soften on kneading. The softness and longer drying time allows time for modelling detail and creating a smoother finish.

In this type of modelling, moulds are used for faces and torsos, to give a realistic effect which can be refined with detail for the particular model being made.

Support Stand

I use a support stand, see page 45, when modelling figures, leaving both hands free for intricate work and reducing the risk of damaging the figure. This is made from two lengths of wooden cake dowels positioned in a block of styrofoam. A piece of 26 gauge wire is wound around and between the dowels to form a noose which supports the neck of the figure. I also find this stand useful for transporting figures.

▼ An *artists' model, used to show figure proportions and positions.*

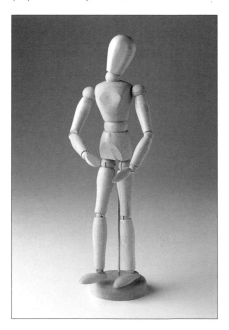

Flower Girl Figurine

◆ About 185g (6 oz) Modelling Paste, see page 8
◆ About 125g (4 oz) Flower Paste, see page 8
◆ 30 g (1 oz) sugarpaste

This figurine illustrates the techniques employed when modelling figures in detail. The flower girl is featured on the Walk in The Park cake, see page 64.

Forming the Torso – Using Head Moulds

The torso is formed in modelling paste using head moulds. The modelling paste must be supple and free from cracks.

Lightly dust the mould with cornflour (corn starch). Shape the paste into a cylinder and push it firmly into the mould, ensuring

> ### MODELLING MEMO
>
> *When modelling the top torso leave the cocktail stick (toothpick) in place when attaching it to the lower torso. This will make the model stronger. If you are entering a competition or which non-edible supports are not permitted, the cocktail stick has to be removed. Ensure that you allow plenty of time for the figure to dry before transporting it.*

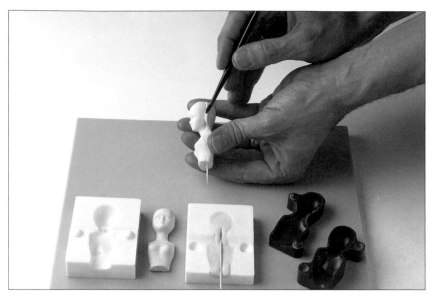

▲ *Using a head mould.*

that the paste is pushed firmly into the face section so that the contours of the nose are clearly impressed in it. Trim the surplus paste from the edge of the mould with a small cranked palette knife. Release the model from the mould.

Repeat this process with the back section of the mould. Insert a cocktail stick (toothpick) into the back section and brush the paste with sugar glue. Secure the front of the model to the portion in the back part of the mould. Carefully release the model completely from the back section of the mould.

▼ *Painting eye details.*

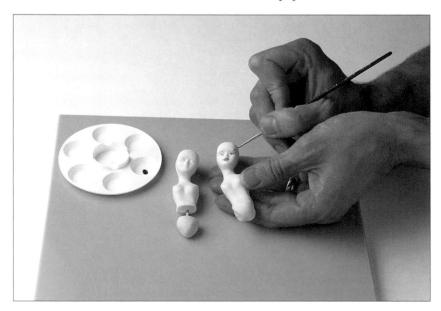

Smooth the join between the front and back portions of the model, then stand the head in a piece of styrofoam and adjust the pose. Leave to dry for 24 hours.

The photograph shows two alternative types of mould, both giving similar results. Moulds can be obtained for male and female characters.

Eyelids and Lower Torso

Moisten the join between the back and front of the model and smooth small pieces of skin tone paste over it, smoothing the edges with a dresden tool.

Form the eyelids from very small pieces of paste and secure on the eye with sugar glue. Shape the eyelid with the wide end of a dresden tool. Paint the white of the eye with powder food colouring mixed with a little clear alcohol: apply two coats. Paint the eye with a mixture of blue and white powder food colouring with a hint of black

> ### MODELLING MEMO
>
> *If the surface of the paste begins to dry and crack slightly as you are modelling, work a little white vegetable fat (shortening) onto the surface.*

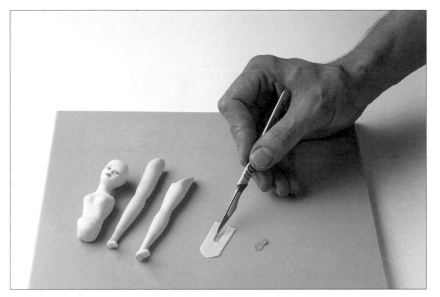

▲ *Making shoes.*

added to produce the blue-grey colour. When painting the eyes, note the direction in which the figure is looking. Paint the pupils, leaving a small section unpainted so that it can be highlighted with white to give a light-reflection effect. Dilute skin tone colour with alcohol and use a no. I paintbrush to brush it over the eyelid. Paint a fine line of black over the edge of the eyelid. Paint a darker brown for the eye brows.

Brush the cheeks with skin tone powder food colouring but take care not to use too much colour.

Remove the cocktail stick from the torso, see Modelling Memo, left, by gently twisting it as you pull it from the paste. Model the lower part of the torso from a sphere of skin tone paste. Shape the leg sockets, then leave to dry on a piece of foam sponge, allowing the lower part to overhang so that it does not flatten during drying.

Legs

The leg and foot should be equal in length to the complete torso. Shape the legs one by one from cylinders of paste. Roll the paste on the edge of your little finger to form the knee and ankle joints. Pull the paste forward and shape the foot, using the dresden tool to shape the ankle and the toes. If

the figure has bare feet, then use a scalpel to mark the toes. Shape the top part of the leg by forming it against the leg socket of the torso. Repeat for the other leg, taking care to shape the foot in the correct direction. Allow to dry for 24 hours.

Shoes

Roll out a little pink paste thinly. Trim the paste as shown and cut a section from the middle. Brush the top and sides of the foot with sugar glue, then position the paste over the foot, forming the join at the back. Cut off the excess at the

back and around the base of the shoe with scissors.

Roll out a piece of brown paste for the sole, making it slightly thicker at one end to form the heel. Brush the base of the foot with sugar glue, stand it on the brown paste and cut around it with a scalpel. Mark the sole of the shoe, then cut the sides and front part of the shoe to give more shape. Leave to dry. Pink food colouring can be brushed on the paste to shade the shoe. Make the second shoe in the same way.

Hair

Mix a little more sugarpaste into the modelling paste for the hair so that it dries out more slowly, allowing more time to texture the paste. Roll the paste thinly into a rectangle large enough to cover

▼ *Applying hair.*

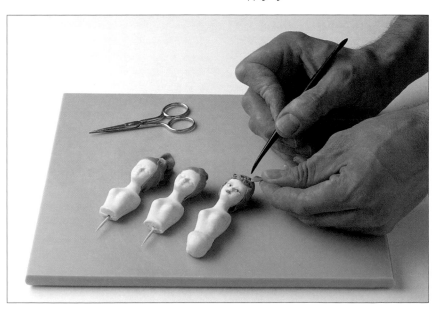

the head. Brush the head with sugar glue, taking care not to brush below the hair line. Place the rectangle of paste over the head and carefully mould it to shape. Trim the excess with scissors.

Flatten small pieces of paste between your fingers. Brush a small area of the head with sugar glue and apply the flattened piece of paste. Texture this using the pointed end of a dresden tool. Small cuts can also be made into the paste with a scalpel but ensure that you make the cuts in the direction in which the hair grows. Continue adding small sections of paste until the head is completely covered, then allow to dry. Shade the hair with powder food colouring.

When making hair for a man, follow the first stage and then cut around the ear shape with a scalpel. Continue to texture the paste with a dresden tool. For a male figurine, small pieces of modelling paste should be used to model ears and these should be secured to the head with sugar glue before adding the hair, particularly if the ears are to show.

Attaching the Legs

Have the support stand ready. Roll a small cylinder of skin tone paste and brush sugar glue around the top of the leg. Push the cylinder of paste between the leg and the body, smoothing down the paste as you work to secure the leg to the body. Repeat for the other leg. Stand the figure in the support stand and allow to dry for 24 hours.

Arms and Hands

Roll a cylinder length for each arm, long enough to reach from the top of the shoulder to the top of the thigh. Roll the paste on the edge of your little finger to form the wrist joint and elbow. Rub white vegetable fat on the joints to bend them and prevent the paste from cracking later.

▲ *Attaching the legs.*

Shape the paste with your thumb and index finger to form the hand. Cut a 'V' shape with the scalpel for the thumb and make three more cuts to form the fingers. Make a small 'V' cut between each finger. Gently roll the cut edge of each finger between your thumb and index finger or use two dresden tools, one in each hand, to shape the fingers.

Model the top of the arm and position it against the shoulder in the pose required. Repeat for the

▼ *Cutting the paste to form fingers.*

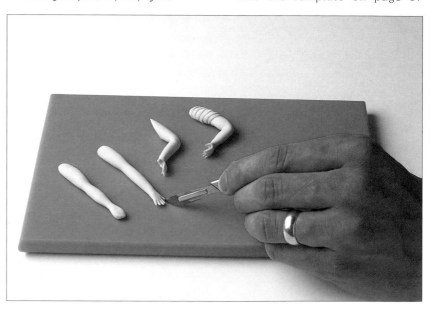

other arm, working the opposite way around. Allow to dry for 12 hours. Paint the finger nails with a pale pink/skin tone colour using a no. 1 paintbrush.

Dressing the Figure

Underskirt Colour 30g (1 oz) flower paste very pale pink. Roll it out thinly into a rectangle measuring 14 x 7cm (5½ x 2¾ in). Frill one long edge for the bottom of the skirt and pleat the opposite edge to fit around the waist of the figure. Brush the pleated edge with sugar glue and attach it around the waist of the figure. Neaten the edge with a scalpel.

Top, Skirt and Bodice Colour 45g (1½ oz) flower paste a darker pink and 45g (1½ oz) a pale mauve. Roll out the paste thinly. Cut out the front and back bodice from the pink paste and use the open end of a piping tube (tip) to cut the neckline for the back. Cut the curved neckline for the front with a scalpel. I find it easier to cut a piece of paste to the approximate size, then hold it against the figure and mark the length of the bodice on it before trimming to the exact size. Secure the bodice with sugar glue, ensuring that the edges of the neckline are not flat against the torso.

Use the template on page 67

for the skirt section, lay it on the paste and cut it out with a scalpel. Cut out two sections each in pink and mauve. Roll a piece of thin tapered dowel across a section of paste to give it texture. Lightly soften the cut edges with a ball tool. Brush the waist of the figure with sugar glue, then work from the right applying the section at an angle. Continue applying the sections in alternate colours.

To make the waist band, roll a mixture of the pink and mauve paste thinly. Cut a 5mm (¼ in) wide band measuring 8cm (3½ in) long. Mark lines on the paste with the veining end of a dresden tool. Brush the back of the band with sugar glue and attach it around the waist, trimming excess and making the join at the back.

Sleeves When the arms have dried the sleeves can be added. Roll out pink paste thinly and cut five 5mm x 3 cm (¼ x 1¼ in) and one 8 x 5mm (⅓ x ¼ in) bands. Brush the back of each band with sugar glue in turn and position around the arm. Trim the surplus paste with small scissors, ensuring all seams are on the underneath of the arm. Continue overlapping the bands and finish with the larger piece at the top, forming the edge at the top of the arm. Cut a small

▲ *Attaching the arms.*

section out of the paste to allow for the join between the arm and the body. Allow to dry for 2 – 3 hours.

Attaching the Arms
Take a small piece of paste the same colour as the dress. Brush the arm socket with sugar glue and position the paste in it. Brush the arm with sugar glue and gently apply pressure as you attach it to the body, neatening the edge with a dresden tool. Make sure that the pose is correct and repeat on

▼ *Making the basket of flowers.*

the other arm. Leave to dry for 12 hours.

Neck Frill
Roll out pink flower paste thinly and cut a 13cm x 5mm (5 x ¼ in) strip. Frill both long edges of the strip. Mark down the middle with the veining end of a dresden tool. Brush the back with sugar glue and attach the frill just below the neckline of the dress, making the join at the back of the figure. Cut a bow shape piece of paste with a scalpel and bring the two ends to the centre, securing them with sugar glue. Cut a small piece of paste to form the middle of the bow. Attach the bow to the dress.

Completing the Figurine
To complete the figurine, add a bow at the back of the waist and brush the edges of the skirt with a little powder food colouring to emphasize the colour.

Basket of Flowers
Make a small basket of flowers from a small cone of brown flower paste, gradually enlarging it by opening it out with your finger and thumb. Use a dresden tool to shape the bottom, then trim the top edge of the basket using a small pair of scissors. Roll a small piece of paste into a thin cylinder shape, fold it in half and twist it to form the handle. Curve this around so that the ends fit on opposite sides of the basket and secure both ends onto the inside of the basket with sugar glue.

Colour flower paste a dark green and roll it out thinly. Cut strands with the scalpel and allow them to dry. Colour the flower paste for the flowers, then shape small cones of different colours on the ends of cocktail sticks (toothpicks) and allow to dry. For the roses, flatten a small piece of paste very thinly on one edge. Place a cocktail stick on the opposite edge and roll up the paste tightly to form the centre of

Making Moulds

You can make your own moulds from a source such as a porcelain figure. The mould can be made by imprinting the face of the figure into flower paste. Leave the paste to dry for 2 – 3 days by which time the impression of the face will be firmly set. Then you can use the mould as you would use a bought one.

To make a longer-lasting mould, different modelling clays and liquid latex can be purchased from craft suppliers and art shops. Lightly grease the face of the porcelain figure with white vegetable fat (shortening) and press the face into the modelling clay. Follow the manufacturer's instructions for setting the modelling material – this will make a permanent mould. To use the mould, press the modelling paste into it, ensuring you push the paste into the nose area on a face mould. When the face is fully dry, form a cylinder of modelling paste and shape the torso and neck of the figure. Make the half-head shape for the back of the head and secure the dry face to it with sugar glue. Smooth the two joints, then allow the head and torso to dry on a piece of foam sponge.

▼ *Making a head mould.*

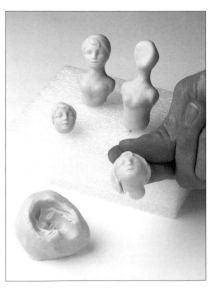

a rose. Very small petals can be added to make an open rose. Dust with powder food colouring when dry. Fill a piping bag fitted with a no. 0 piping tube (tip) with royal icing coloured a contrasting green. Position the green strands of paste in the basket, securing with the green icing. Pipe small beads of icing down the green strands to look like leaves, pulling the bag away as you pipe to give the leaf shape. Use a small pair of tweezers to attach the small flowers to the leaves with the green icing.

Displaying the Figurine

The figurine is attached to a pastillage plaque with a mixture of flower paste and a little sugar glue on the soles of her shoes. The figure is held in the support frame for 24 hours until the paste and glue are dry before being moved. The plaque fits into the base of the Walk in The Park cake, see page 64.

PLANNING A MODEL

The extent to which you have to plan a model depends on the size of the project. If you follow the ideas in the chapter of Models on Cakes, see page 56, it is not necessary to make any separate plans as all the templates and instructions are provided. The idea of this book is to provide more than a set number of completed cakes. The animals and characters in the opening chapters show how basic skills are used and the finished items can be used individually as cake decorations; they can also be used to make a more complicated model, as shown in this section. The same applies to models in the cake designs – many can be used as part of a different scene.

The Theme

First you have to establish the theme for the model. Collect source material on the theme so that you can build up the idea and decide exactly on what the model should be. Post cards, magazine cuttings and photographs are all useful background information. Draw rough sketches of real life objects if you like, to get some idea of scale and how they will look together in a model. When you have a broad range of ideas, select one or two which you find most suitable and which you can imagine working in sugarcraft modelling. Sometimes a clear idea evolves at this stage but more often than not the ideas change as you investigate the techniques which you can use.

Occasions and Colours

The majority of cakes and sugarcraft work is prepared for specific occasions and celebrations – a wedding, christening, birthday, anniversary, retirement and so on.

▲ *Developing the idea for a model, using inspirational material as well as suitable backgrounds and the part-made figure.*

The occasion is the first consideration when making a cake. When planning a model, it is a good idea to think of a suitable theme and then to establish the link with the occasion. For example, it may be possible to colour coordinate the theme of your model with the occasion; for a wedding this is usually an important priority.

Using colours which match lifelike items is not always necessary nor suitable for models, and it depends on the extent to which the model is meant to look like the real thing or to be an artistic impression of it. Whenever you plan a model, consider the preferences of the recipient: some subjects have to be modelled in realistic colours to make an authentic impression and the colours may not be the best for the occasion. Being aware of such points will ensure that your model is the perfect centrepiece.

Composition

When the model is more than a single item, the composition of the scene is important. A model can be made as a tableau, usually a project which is never intended

as a cake decoration but made for exhibition or competition work. More often, the model is made to complement a cake; in this case the model may be the main focus or it may play a vital supporting role in the overall design, for example as in the modelled flower pedestal on the Water Maiden cake, see page 112.

Using some models solely as a cake-top decoration is fine for a very simple design, for example on a child's birthday cake, but they always look more interesting when both cake and model together form a complete scene. This means that the design of cake and the models used on top – or on the side – have to be planned as one. I have used this technique for all the cakes featured in this book, in the hope that it will inspire you to plan themes of your own as well as making individual items. If you do not want to create the whole scene, the instructions for separate items can be followed and you can always adopt part of the idea for a different theme when decorating a cake – the choice is yours.

Techniques for Individual Models

There are various techniques which can be used; different techniques are best suited to different mediums, such as marzipan and pastillage. Read through the first part of the book and look at the basic modelling skills for guidance when planning a model. Remember the limitations of the medium as well as the possibilities it offers. It is possible to adapt the various skills to the different modelling materials once you are used to working with them.

Size

If the model is to go on top of a cake, the size of the cake will dictate the dimensions of the model. Proportions and scale should be clearly defined. Taking the Gardening cake, page 78, as an example, the model of the gardener was made first as it is larger and a more important point of focus than the wheelbarrow. The gardener then provided a guide for the size of the wheelbarrow. A rough sketch of the wheelbarrow was made from a life-size barrow – this is always a good starting point. The sketch was simplified for the model and drawn down to the right size. The wheelbarrow was constructed from sections of pastillage, so the next stage in planning the model was making a cardboard template.

Making a Template

More than one template may have to be cut for any single item. When planning a scene with several models, as shown on the cakes in this book, take care to plan the different items in proportion to each other.

Taking the same cake as an example, the wheelbarrow was planned to fit the dimensions of the gardener by comparing a life-size barrow alongside a living person. Once the sketch looked right in proportion to a person, I was able to reduce it to the size of the gardener. When the overall proportion is correct, each section should be sketched and traced on thin card. At this stage it is a good idea to cut out and assemble the sections if possible – the wheelbarrow sections were easily joined with adhesive tape. Any which did not fit were cut again, at a slightly different angle. This method saves time and ensures that the pieces will fit together securely when they are cut in modelling paste and allowed to dry.

Consider the thickness of the paste compared to that of the card template. If the sections should be thicker than the cardboard template, either allow for the thickness when you plan the width of the sections or use thicker cardboard to make the template.

Practical Considerations

The design should be practical for sugar modelling as you must be able to transport it – if only for lifting onto the cake, then moving it. There is no point in making a model which is so delicate that one jolt will cause the whole thing to collapse.

Unless you are making an exact replica of an object and working to scale plans, it is far less frustrating and more fun to invent a particular style. Take artistic licence and use your imagination – you may even develop your own modelling techniques. Many established cake decorators have their own style of modelling in sugar which is easily recognized at sugarcraft exhibitions.

Finishing Touches

Detail always attracts attention and makes a model visually interesting quite simply because there is more to look at. Sometimes the scale of an item can make it appealing, for example when preparing miniature pieces. The novel way in which many models are displayed can distinguish them and provide unique appeal as well as a platform for displaying various techniques and skills.

Storing Sugarcraft Models

The advantage of a model decoration on a cake is that it can be preserved as a keepsake of a special occasion. By displaying the model in a suitable container or glass cabinet, it will be protected from moisture and dust. If you have spent long hours creating a masterpiece, it is worth investing in one of the many purpose-made containers or display cabinets, often sold complete with suitable plinths on which to display a model.

Pastillage and flower paste models do not have to be sealed with any special glaze or fixative; to preserve the appearance of the model, avoid placing it in strong sunlight as many of the food colourings will fade. A dry atmosphere is also important for successful storage, as humidity will cause the model to sag and become distorted. In the right conditions, a model will keep well for many years.

Tableaux

A tableau is a display piece, usually made to commission by professional sugarcraft workers, for competition or exhibition purposes. However, a tableau can also be designed as a gift to commemorate a special occasion. A tableau can be made to any size; a small scene may be the perfect celebration gift but one which is intended for a competition must comply with the base area stipulated in the requirements set out for entrants.

Selecting a Theme

Unless you are going to make a replica of an existing model or life-size object, the first step is to gather sources of inspiration and information. This is much the same as preparing a simpler model but it involves more in-depth research to build up a complete scene with all aspects harmonizing. Books, cards, photographs and everyday objects are all important sources.

Entering a Competition

Study the rules until you are quite clear about the requirements and understand the ways in which they can be interpreted. If the rules allow the use of non-edible internal supports, then you will be able to use items inside the model to support it if you wish, for example wooden dowel. Some competitions state that only edible internal supports are permitted, in which case wood, metal and any other inedible material must be avoided. Failure to comply with the rules of a competition usually leads to disqualification.

Once you have a clear idea of what you can and cannot use, you can plan the tableau around your chosen theme, and think about the techniques you will use for each part as you build up the idea.

Displaying a Tableau

Selecting a board to complement the theme improves the overall presentation. Although cake boards are suitable, they can limit the choice of shape, so it is a good idea to cut a piece of plywood to the required size and cover it with cake board foil.

When entering a competition, keep the board within the maximum size. If you are allowed to use non-edible internal supports, you can build a base to act as a background for the sugarcraft work, as shown in the Happy New Year project, see page 53, where the back of the

house and balcony are cut from plywood. Alternatively, sections can be cut from marzipan reinforced with gum tragacanth, as shown in the caravan on page 133.

When planning a scene around a limited angle, for example in a 90° corner as part of a room or in a semi-circular curve, parts of the model will require close attention to detail to make it interesting. A 360°, all-round, view provides many interesting aspects and new features can always be discovered by looking at the scene from a different angle. The detail is evenly distributed throughout the work rather than concentrated on areas which may otherwise appear flat and uninteresting.

A Country Scene, see page 56.

Japanese Garden

This model shows how spaghetti can be used as a support when modelling with marzipan (almond paste) strengthened with gum tragacanth. For competition purposes, spaghetti is an edible product. The black perspex (plexiglass) base was chosen to create the effect of reflections on water and to show that different materials can be used as a base for sugarcraft models. Most sugarcraft suppliers will be able to advise on where to obtain bases of this type, cut to any requirements. The template for the shape is on page 52.

Marzipan

The complete model required 1.24kg (2½ lb) marzipan (almond paste) and 15 pieces of spaghetti. The marzipan was coloured first as described on page 12. Icing (confectioners') sugar was then kneaded into the marzipan for the figure to make it white, with care not to make the paste too dry.

The Figure

Planning the figure as part of the design is important; the expression and stance must be planned to fit in with the surroundings.

Head

Use a model as a guide when shaping the head and follow the sequence shown for the gardener on page 81. Shape the hair and make two small holes in it so that the headdress can be added when the paste is dry. Make the hair in sections, joining each piece together neatly.

Body

Add gum tragacanth in the proportion of 5ml (1 teaspoon) to 250g (8 oz) marzipan (almond paste) for the body. Use the diagram on page 52 as a guide to proportions for head to body when shaping the body. Insert four

lengths of spaghetti down through the centre of the body before attaching the head as shown on page 81, for the gardener. Stand the figure on a small rolling board, ready to continue the modelling. To prevent the mar-zipan from drying out too quickly, cut the top off a plastic bottle and use it to cover the figure. Then leave the figure to set for 24 hours before adding the clothes.

Dressing the Figure and Adding Arms

The kimono is made from thinly rolled marzipan, with a lighter colour lining underneath and darker paste on top for each section. Fit the lining first. Cut a rectangle of thinly rolled paste long enough for the body and wrap it around the figure, up and over the shoulders. Trim the paste to fit. The technique for making arms is shown on page 44. Cut two separate rectangles for sleeves and wrap them around the arms.

Completing the Figure

Once the figure has arms and a dress, add details to the hair and cut out a marzipan fan using the template on page 52. Secure the fan to the hand with a paste made from marzipan (almond paste) mixed with sugar glue. The decoration on the hair is made from marzipan with a little gum tragacanth added. Secure the figure to the perspex base with the same marzipan and sugar glue paste.

Garden

Several stages of rough sketches and a good deal of research among books and photographic sources was necessary before the design was determined.

Bamboo

Mix 250g (8 oz) marzipan (almond paste) with 5ml (1 teaspoon) gum tragacanth and colour it brown. Cut lengths of spaghetti ranging from 10cm (4 in) to 25cm (10 in). Roll pieces of marzipan into small cylinders, then insert lengths of spaghetti into them. Continue rolling the marzipan gently until it completely covers the spaghetti.

Mark notches at intervals around the bamboo by rolling it on the thin edge of a palette knife and make two small marks on either side of the notches. Place the length of bamboo on a piece of foam sponge. Lift the sponge slightly at one end and support it so that the bamboo dries with a slight curve.

For variation in colour between the bamboo canes, mix a little green marzipan with the brown when some of the canes have been shaped. Repeat the modelling process and leave the bamboo to dry for 1 week.

Leaves Make leaves for the bamboo as shown in the photograph on page 50. Secure these around the bamboo with a little sugar glue and smooth down their edges. Support each cane of bamboo in a tall glass until all are completed.

Arranging the bamboo on the base Take about 185g (6 oz) green marzipan (almond paste) and shape it into a smooth mound. Place this on the section of the black base, see template page 52, and texture it as for grass, see page 39. Make deep indents for the pieces of bamboo, then arrange each piece carefully in the marzipan. You may find it easier to place the black base on a piece of polystyrene, then support the pieces of bamboo with lengths of 24-gauge wire, pushed into the polystyrene. Leave the bamboo on its base to set for 5 days before moving it.

Bridge

Use marzipan (almond paste) strengthened with gum tragacanth, see page 9, for amounts, and roll it out to 5mm (¼ in) thick. Using the template on page 52, cut out the rectangle for the bridge. Lay this over a half section of drain pipe to dry in a curve and leave for 24 hours. Lift the section off, turn the pipe over and lay the marzipan in it to dry the other side of the curve. Leave for 24 hours. Repeat the process of turning the marzipan until it is hard – this will take about 5 days.

Railings Roll lengths of marzipan as for the bamboo and insert pieces of spaghetti in them. Dry these flat on a piece of foam sponge.

Assembling the bridge Lay the bridge on its side on a sheet of paper and trace the curve of the marzipan. Remove the bridge and use the curve as a guide for assembling the railings, positioning them on paper, and radiating from the curve. Then replace the bridge. When you are sure that the positions are correct, use a mixture of marzipan and sugar glue as a paste on each of the railings to secure them to the bridge. Place the handrail in position next and secure it with the marzipan and sugar glue mixture. Leave the bridge on its side for about 24 hours, or until firmly set. Repeat the process to attach the railings and handrail to the other side of the bridge. Support the dry railings and handrail with a piece of foam sponge while the second side is being positioned.

When completely dry, position the bridge on the black base, securing it with small amounts of soft marzipan and a little sugar glue.

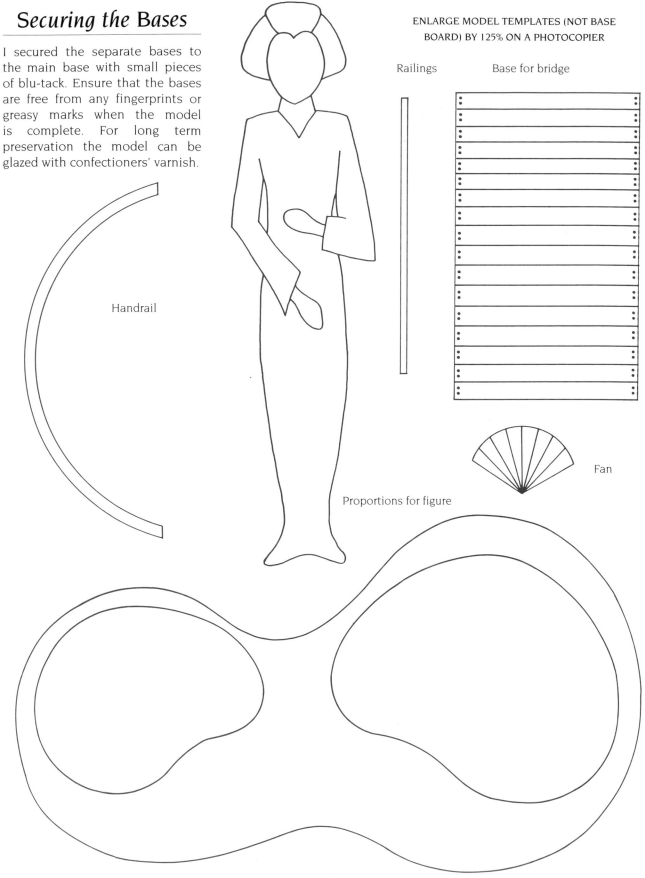

Securing the Bases

I secured the separate bases to the main base with small pieces of blu-tack. Ensure that the bases are free from any fingerprints or greasy marks when the model is complete. For long term preservation the model can be glazed with confectioners' varnish.

ENLARGE MODEL TEMPLATES (NOT BASE BOARD) BY 125% ON A PHOTOCOPIER

Railings

Base for bridge

Handrail

Fan

Proportions for figure

Base boards: lower and two upper boards
ENLARGE TO GIVE BASE LENGTH OF 45CM (16 IN)

Happy New Year Tableau

This tableau shows just how detailed sugarcraft modelling can be. It needed 16kg (32 lb) marzipan (almond paste) and I spent four weeks working on it. If you do not feel sufficiently confident to tackle a large project, have a go at one small aspect of the scene. All the characters are modelled individually and basic instructions with step-by-step illustrations show how they are made, see pages 29 to 38.

Marzipan

Raw marzipan (almond paste) was used, along with added icing (confectioners') sugar and liquid glucose (clear corn syrup), following the recipe on page 9. For the complete tableau you will need 16kg (32 lb) marzipan, and it should be coloured before you begin to model.

The Base and Background

The plywood base measures 45.5cm (18 in) square. First the back wall was constructed on both sides, then the pillars for the balcony were made from wooden dowel and covered with marzipan. The spiral effect was modelled using the handle of a modelling tool.

Flooring

The strips of flooring for the inside of the house were cut from marzipan and applied individually. Then small holes for the screws in the floorboards were made and filled with a darker marzipan.

Tree, Paving and Snow

The tree on the outside of the house was modelled in sections, then the joins were blended together so that they did not show. Paving slabs, see page 39, were cut and applied to the floor behind the house. The snow drifts were modelled after the paving.

▲ *The rear of the Happy New Year Tableau shows the outside of the house.*

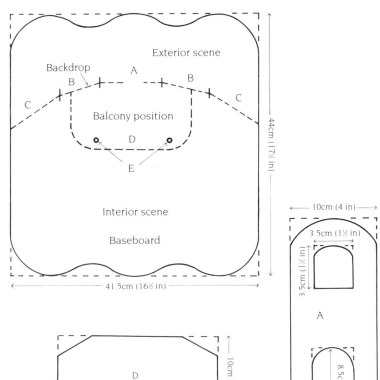

Exterior scene

Backdrop

A

B   B

C   Balcony position   C

D

E

Interior scene

Baseboard

44cm (17½ in)

41.5cm (16½ in)

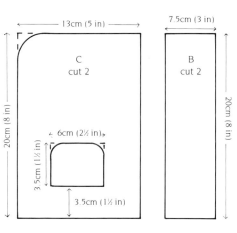

13cm (5 in)

7.5cm (3 in)

C
cut 2

B
cut 2

20cm (8 in)

20cm (8 in)

6cm (2½ in)

3.5cm (1½ in)

3.5cm (1½ in)

Draw rectangles to full size shown
by dotted lines, then add curves
and features

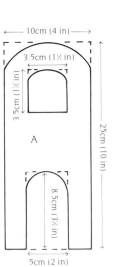

10cm (4 in)

3.5cm (1½ in)

3.5cm (1½ in)

A

25cm (10 in)

8.5cm (3¼ in)

5cm (2 in)

D
Balcony

10cm (4 in)

20cm (8 in)

Balcony support

E

8.5cm (3½ in)

2.5cm (1 in)

Door, Railings and Windows

For these the marzipan was strengthened with gum tragacanth, see page 9. The curtain rail was also strengthened with gum tragacanth and allowed to dry before draping the curtains on it.

Building up the Scene

Once the base was started, I had a scale to which the animals and other items had to be modelled. It is important to establish the background and base area first so that the separate pieces all fit into it, and this applies to small pieces with just two or three items as well as to a complicated tableau.

When all the animal characters were in place, they provided a framework in which to add extra items and details. First, all the key characters and items had to be positioned, then, when their places were clear, each item was secured to the base board with a mixture of marzipan and a little sugar glue.

A base board edging was added to the tableau; alternatively, the sides of the board can be covered with marzipan.

Glazing and Storing a Model or Tableau

Marzipan must not be glazed for competitions. A glaze can be applied to preserve a tableau for many years and prevent the colours from fading. The work should be allowed to dry out before glazing. This model was left for 3 months, by which time it was completely dry and very hard. Clear confectioners' glaze was brushed over the surface, carefully applying it to all the tiny items. Three coats were used and each was allowed to dry before the next was added.

A clear display cabinet should be used to protect the model, allowing it to be displayed without getting dirty and dusty. These can be purpose built for large tableaux or purchased ready-made for smaller models; most sugarcraft suppliers will be pleased to advise.

Festive Sing-Along

These jolly characters make an excellent focal point for a smaller tableau or cake-top model. Arrange them on a small base, with or without a background, as you wish. A Christmas tree background or corner complete with yule-tide decorations could be added.

MODELS ON CAKES

A Country Scene

This cake shows how the shape of the cake is used to create perspective for the model. Instead of placing the model on top of the cake, a wider view is created by cutting the cake to form a backdrop for the model of a house. The church in the background contributes to the feeling of space and distance. The idea was built up from a walk in the country, a good way of thinking up a theme for a model.

INGREDIENTS

23cm (9 in) round cake
Apricot Glaze, see page 14
1kg (2 lb) marzipan (almond paste)
315g (10 oz) Pastillage 1 or 2, see
    page 8
selection of food colourings
clear alcohol (vodka or gin)
1.25kg (2½ lb) sugarpaste
30g (1 oz) Flower Paste, see
    page 8
small amount of royal icing

EQUIPMENT

30cm (12 in) round cake board
tilting turntable
dresden tool
fine emery board
paintbrushes
flat chisel paintbrush
plain piping tube (tip)
greaseproof paper (parchment)
    piping bag
wire brush

▲ Drying the background.

Leave in this position to dry for 12 hours.

While the blue pastillage is drying, colour 90g (3 oz) pastillage cream for the house and roll it out to 1mm (¹⁄₁₆ in) thick. Use the templates to cut out the house sections. Place on a drying board to dry hard, turning occasionally.

Remove the blue background from the cake after 12 hours and transfer it to a drying board so that the air can circulate around it. Cut the second background section. Replace the first section in the curve of the cake, then position the second section on top. Allow to dry for 12 hours before removing from the cakes.

Brush the cake with clear alcohol and cover it with sugarpaste. Mark lines for the fields in the soft paste using the veining end of a dresden tool. Using pastillage left from the house, cut out the church. Dry this in a curve which corresponds to the shape of the field.

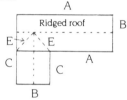

▼ The cut sections, including the base.

Use the diagram, see page 59, as a guide for cutting the cake. Brush the cake with apricot glaze, cover it with marzipan, see page 14, smoothing it neatly over the curves and into the side. Leave to dry.

Cut out all the templates for the model in thin card, see page 59. Colour 90g (3 oz) pastillage pale blue for the house background, then roll it out to 1.5mm (¾ in) thick. Cut out the house background using the templates. Place the cake on the tilting turntable and tilt it away from you. Place a piece of thin card in the cut-out curve of the cake. Lift the background section of blue pastillage on the template and position it in the curve of the cake.

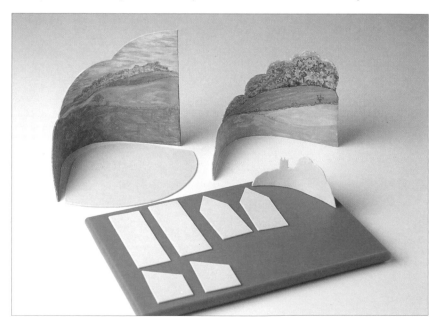

Cutting a Base

When sections for the house and its background are thoroughly dry, sand down any rough edges with a fine emery board. Use cream pastillage for the base and roll it out to 1.5mm (generous ¹⁄₁₆ in) thick. Place the larger background section on the base and use it as a guide for cutting the pastillage. Use the template to cut the front.

Painting the Background

It is difficult to trace onto a curved surface and the pastillage is quite likely to break if too much pressure is applied. Use a soft pencil to outline the hills. Paint the sky first, then paint the hills before adding fine detail. Use a large paintbrush to avoid excessive brushing on the

pastillage. If the surface is over-brushed the sugar dissolves.

Assembling the House

Trace the windows onto the house sections. Colour the house with powder food colouring using a flat chisel paintbrush. Paint on the windows and the occasional area of detail for brickwork.

Roll out a small piece of flower paste thinly and cut out narrow strips to reinforce the joins between sections of the house. Before joining two sections, cut strips of paste slightly shorter than the edges of the sections and attach them with sugar glue. Assemble adjacent sections as shown, supporting the pieces as necessary with small pieces of foam sponge until dry. Gradually build up the house, allowing each join to dry before making another.

Join both roof sections together and place on the house until dry. Spoon a little royal icing coloured the same as the house into a piping bag fitted with a plain piping tube (tip) and pipe a line down the gable ends. Remove any excess icing with a damp brush. Fill any gaps between the paste sections with royal icing.

Model the chimney stacks from flower paste and leave until partly dried. Cut a 'V' shape in the base of the stacks so that they fit neatly on top of the house. Roll a thin strand of flower paste and leave to part dry, then cut off small pieces to make chimney pots. Secure the pots to the chimney stacks with sugar glue. Allow to dry completely before painting the detail on the chimneys.

▲ *Support the house sections with foam sponge as they are assembled.*

Completing and Assembling the Model

Stand the house on the base and draw an outline around it, then set it aside. Paint the path and grass. Make the hedge from small pieces of flower paste and texture them with a wire brush. Leave the hedge to dry before painting it.

Fence

For the fence, roll out a small piece of flower paste thinly and cut short lengths for the posts. Cut two longer strips, brush with sugar glue and lay them across the posts. Leave the fence to dry completely before painting it on both sides.

Gate

Make the gate by cutting 5 strips of thinly rolled flower paste. Attach 2 strips at the ends with sugar glue. Attach 2 strips in a 'V' shape in the middle of the gate and a further single strip down the middle. Paint on both sides with food colouring when dry.

▼ *Assembling the model.*

Assembling the model

Pipe a line of royal icing along the back curved edge of the base and place the large piece of background in position on it. Attach the smaller curved section in front of it with royal icing – this is the middle ground. Make sure that the painted view is displayed to best advantage when fixing the pieces in place.

Secure the house to the base with royal icing before adding the hedge, gate and fence, fixing them all securely. Leave the complete model to dry thoroughly before placing it on the board with the cake. Complete the decoration by piping very tiny dots of deep mauve royal icing on the mauve-coloured fields and green royal icing between the fields. Then use a small paintbrush to texture the surface slightly.

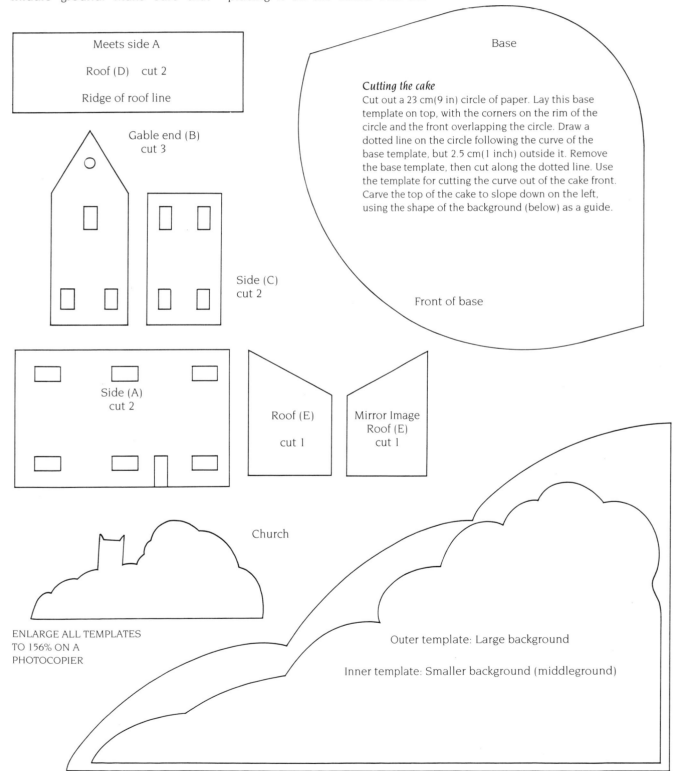

Meets side A

Roof (D)   cut 2

Ridge of roof line

Gable end (B)
cut 3

Side (C)
cut 2

Side (A)
cut 2

Roof (E)

cut 1

Mirror Image
Roof (E)

cut 1

Base

Cutting the cake
Cut out a 23 cm(9 in) circle of paper. Lay this base template on top, with the corners on the rim of the circle and the front overlapping the circle. Draw a dotted line on the circle following the curve of the base template, but 2.5 cm(1 inch) outside it. Remove the base template, then cut along the dotted line. Use the template for cutting the curve out of the cake front. Carve the top of the cake to slope down on the left, using the shape of the background (below) as a guide.

Front of base

Church

ENLARGE ALL TEMPLATES
TO 156% ON A
PHOTOCOPIER

Outer template: Large background

Inner template: Smaller background (middleground)

Anna

This simple cake shows how flat models can be used. The Victorian-style card used on the top of the cake is complemented by flat-pieces of the little girl around the sides. The particular design shown is ideal for a young girl who dreams of owning her own horse but the scene painted on the inside of the card can reflect any other occasion. Remember to pick up on the chosen theme when painting the sides of the cake.

INGREDIENTS

20cm (8 in) hexagonal cake
Apricot Glaze, see page 14
750g (1½ lb) marzipan (almond
    paste)
clear alcohol (vodka or gin)
1.25kg (2½ lb) sugarpaste
selection of food colourings
75g (3 oz) Pastillage 1 or 2, see
    page 8
a little royal icing
75g (3 oz) Flower Paste, see page 8

EQUIPMENT

30cm (12 in) hexagonal cake board
scalloped edge straight frill cutter
nos. 1 and 2 piping tubes (tips)
clear plastic file wallet
dresden tool
piece of plastic guttering (drainpipe)
emery board
fine, medium and 1cm (½ in) flat
    chisel paintbrushes
masking tape
airbrush
greaseproof paper (parchment)
    piping bag
1.5m (5 ft) of 1cm (½ in) wide pink
    ribbon
30cm (12 in) of 1.5mm (⅛ in) wide
    pink ribbon

Brush the cake with apricot glaze and cover it with marzipan, see page 14. Brush with clear alcohol and cover with 875g (1¾ lb) of the sugarpaste, see page 14; leave to dry. Colour the remaining sugarpaste pink and use to cover the cake board, then cut the edge with a scalloped frill cutter.

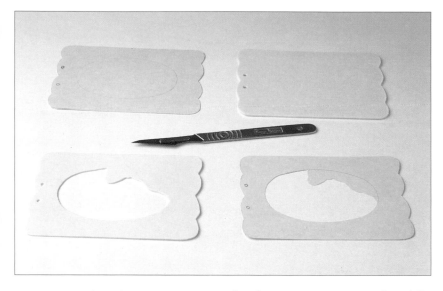

▲ *Cutting out the card.*

Cutting the Card

Trace the card template, see page 63, onto thin card and cut it out. Colour the pastillage pale cream, then roll it out to 1mm (¹⁄₁₆ in) thick. Transfer the pastillage to a drying board, then carefully cut out the card, using a large chopping knife for the straight edges and a scalpel for the intricate areas and middle sections. Use the end of a no. 2 piping tube (tip) to cut the holes for the ribbon at the top of the card. Leave the middle section in place until the card has dried. Leave the card to dry for 24 hours, turning regularly, or until the paste feels hard.

▼ *Making the girl shapes and drying them in a curve over pipe, see page 61.*

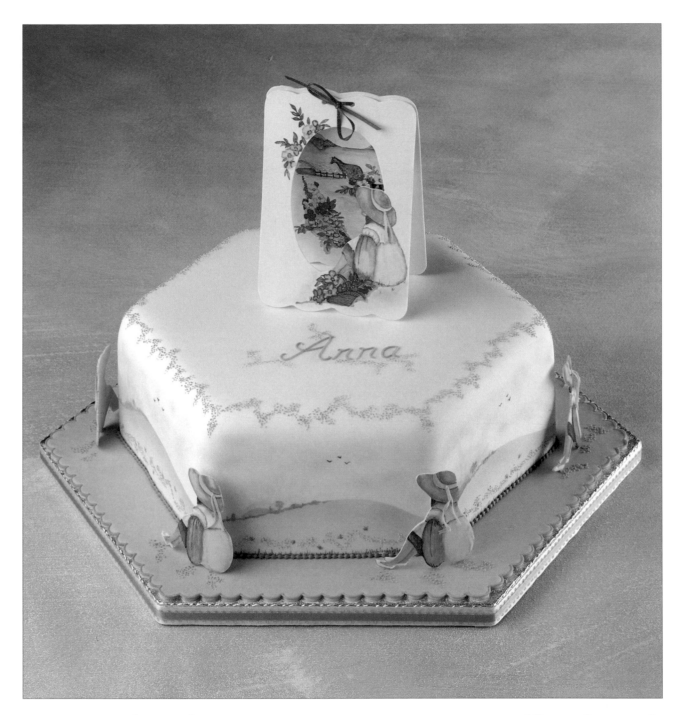

Cutting the Girls

Roll out the flower paste thinly. Trace the girl and place the paper in a clear plastic file wallet. Lay this over the paste and use the veining end of a dresden tool to outline the girl, pressing firmly. Remove the wallet then carefully cut out the girl with a scalpel. Dust a piece of curved guttering pipe with a little cornflour (cornstarch). Carefully lift the girl and lay the paste on the pipe so that it dries in a curve to fit around a corner. Cut out five more shapes and dry for 24 hours.

MODELLING MEMO

It is a good idea to cut extra pieces when making small items like the girls. This will allow for any damage or mishaps when handling and painting the models.

Assembling the Card

Carefully remove any rough edges on the card and girls using a fine emery board. Trace the detail for the front and back of the card and transfer it to the pastillage using a HB pencil.

Use diluted food colouring to paint the background and allow to dry. Then paint the middle ground and allow it to dry before painting on the detail. Use a little white

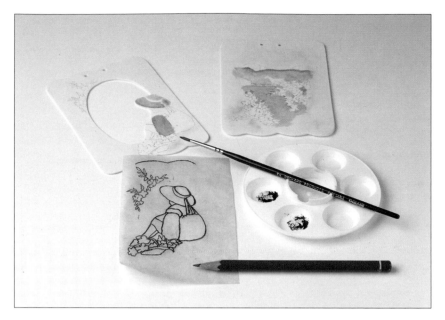

powder food colouring mixed with the liquid food colouring to give a thicker consistency for applying the fine detail. When dry, thread the ribbon through the holes and tie it in a loose bow.

Painting and Supporting the Girls

Paint the detail on the girls to match the card. Colour 15g (½ oz) of the remaining flower paste pale lemon and roll it out thinly. Cut one 2mm x 2cm (⅛ x ⅞ in) strip and one 2mm x 2.5cm (⅛ x 1in) long. Cut a small inverted 'V' in the ends of each piece. Wind the paste around a cocktail stick (toothpick), then remove the stick, leaving the paste twisted. Secure the pieces of paste to the hat on one of the girls with sugar glue. Make ribbons for the remaining hats in the same way.

Completing the Cake

Cut a band of paper to fit around the cake and fold it into six equal sections. Draw a line on the paper to represent the hill on the cake. Cut along the line and reserve both top and bottom of the template. Open the top section and attach it

▲ *Painting the card.*

around the cake, halfway up the sides. Secure it at the join with masking tape.

Airbrush the cake with pale green below the template. Remove the template, then paint the sun just visible over the hill with lemon yellow food colouring. Fix the lower part of the template over the green section to act as a mask and airbrush very pale blue above the

horizon. Paint the trees, grass and birds freehand.

Place the cake on the board. Using a no. 1 piping tube (tip), pipe a bead of green royal icing around the base of the cake. Pipe small clusters of minute dots in green royal icing around the top and base of the cake. This piping is freehand to create a natural and light impression. Scribe a name or greeting on the top of the cake, then over pipe it with soft royal icing, using a no.1 piping tube (tip).

Secure the cut-out girls around the base of the cake with mauve royal icing, placing them 1cm (½ in) from the cake edge. Remove any surplus icing with a damp brush. Pipe minute dots around the girls. Outline the scalloped edge of the board with mauve royal icing.

Trim the board with ribbon, then position the card on top, standing it slightly open. Remove the card while transporting the cake and store it in a flat position.

▼ *The finished card and one of the girls for the cake corners.*

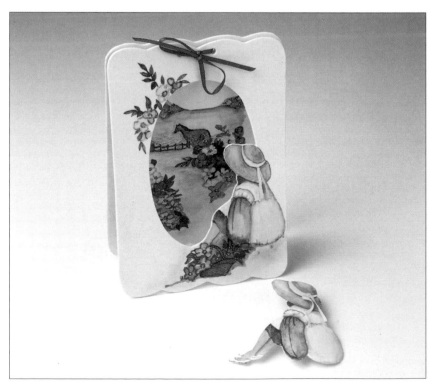

Card back

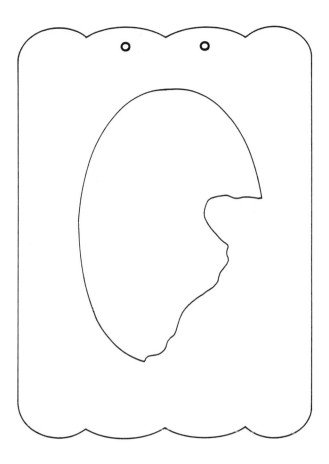

Card front

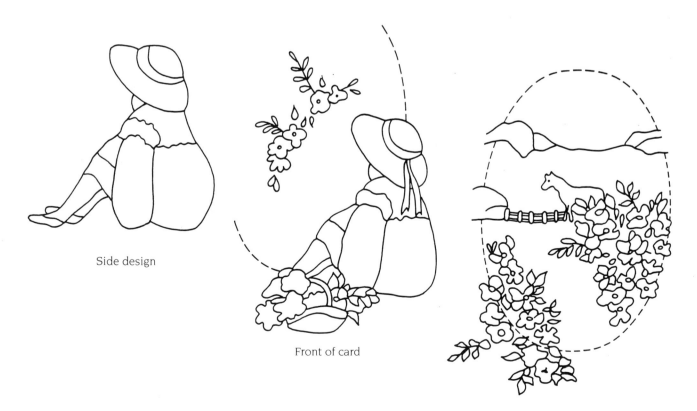

Side design

Front of card

ENLARGE TEMPLATES BY 118% ON A PHOTOCOPIER

Inside design for card

A Walk in the Park

This cake combines the skills of pastillage figurine modelling with marzipan modelling. Perspective is also important in achieving a sense of depth as the cake forms a back drop and a base for the park scene, while the figure is the focal point in the foreground. The figure model can be removed and preserved as a keepsake.

INGREDIENTS

Figurine, see page 42
20cm (8 in) round deep cake
Apricot Glaze, see page 14
750g (1½ lb) marzipan (almond
    paste)
clear alcohol (gin or vodka)
1.75kg (3½ lb) sugarpaste
selection of food colourings
small amount of Royal Icing, see
page 9
125g (4 oz) Pastillage 1 or 2, see
    page 8
250g (8 oz) Modelling Marzipan, see
    page 9
sugar glue or egg white

EQUIPMENT

27.5cm (11 in) round cake board
37.5cm (15 in) oval cake board
medium paintbrush
piece of plastic guttering (drainpipe)
sheet of perspex (plexiglass)
runout film
no. 0 and 2 piping tubes (tips)
dresden tool
cocktail sticks (toothpicks)
spaghetti

Make the figurine following the instructions. She is set on an oval plaque painted in the same way as the paving.

Follow the diagram on page 67 for cutting the cake. Cut a curved section of about a third of the cake. Cut a slice off the curved section to about a quarter of its depth; this slice will be positioned on top of the cake, at the back.

Cut three steep steps in the front of the curved section. Start by cutting a wide strip from the edge to make the top step. Continue cutting strips from the edge of the cake, keeping the curve neat and making the steps narrower each time. Assemble the pieces of cake, using apricot glaze to keep them in place.

Fill any small dents or holes in the cake with marzipan, then brush the cake with apricot glaze and cover with marzipan, see page 14. Colour the sugarpaste pale cream and roll it out to 3mm (⅛ in) thick. Brush the cake with alcohol, then cover it with sugarpaste, see page 14. Take care to smooth the paste neatly over the steps.

Stick the round board on the oval board, towards the back edge, then cover with the remaining sugarpaste rolled out to 4mm (³⁄₁₆ in) thick. Cut out a 10cm (4 in) long oval at the front of the larger board for the figurine. Roll thin cylinders from paste trimmings and flatten them so they have square corners. Lay strips between the steep steps, attaching the paste with alcohol, to make six shallow steps; dry.

Paint the stonework and paving slabs with diluted food colouring, using a mixture of colours, as shown. Light blue, grey, beige and brown are used on the cake, with browns, beige and green on the boards. Attach the cake towards the back of the round board and fill any small spaces between board and cake with cream royal icing.

Gates and Wall

Roll out the pastillage to 1mm (¹⁄₁₆ in) thick. Following the wall template, see page 67, cut the pastillage using a scalpel, and a large kitchen knife for the straight edges. Dry the pieces over the curve of the drain pipe for 12 hours. Paint the stonework pattern on both sides.

Trace the gate template and lay it under a piece of perspex. Cover with runout film and pipe the design using a no. 0 piping tube (tip) and black royal icing. Allow to dry for 24 hours.

▼ *Painting the wall.*

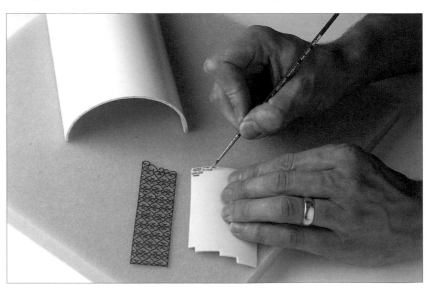

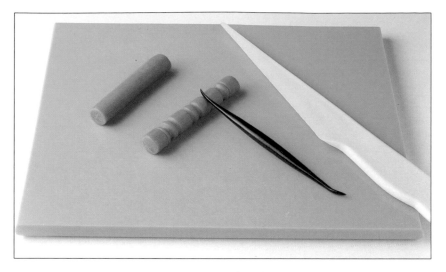

▲ *Making a balustrade.*

Balustrade

Colour two-thirds of the modelling marzipan light brown and the remainder grey, then roll both together to give a marbled effect. Roll the paste into a cylinder and mark rings around it at regular intervals with a dresden tool and the back of a marzipan knife. Cut six 2.5cm (1 in) pieces and six 6cm (2½ in) pieces. Roll the cylinder under the edge of a palette knife until you cut through cleanly without squashing the paste. Dry in a curved tray covered with a polythene bag for 12 hours. When set, insert lengths of spaghetti into the sections for support.

Roll out the marbled marzipan to 4mm (³⁄₁₆ in) thick and use the larger rail template, see page 67, to cut out four pieces. Re-roll the paste trimmings to 3mm (⅛ in) thick and use the top rail template to cut out four pieces. Place on a rolling board, cover with a polythene bag and leave for 12 hours.

Flower Containers

Roll a walnut-sized ball of marbled marzipan, cut it in half, then cup the middle with a ball tool. Mark twelve sections on the outside of the cup with the veining end of a dresden tool. Roll a small cylinder as for the balustrade to make a leg for the container. Cover the pieces with a polythene bag and allow to set for 12 hours.

Assembling the Cake

Secure a pair of large rails for the balustrade to the board and a pair of small rails to the cake with sugar glue. Position the balustrade poles evenly spaced, then attach the top rails.

Use dark green royal icing and a no.1 piping tube (tip) to pipe the creeper on the wall sections. Attach the wall sections to the top of the cake, ensuring that you leave

▼ *Making a flower container.*

a gap 2mm (scant ⅛ in) larger than the width of the gates. Carefully remove the gates from the runout film and secure to the wall sections with black royal icing.

Trailing Wisteria

Make the wisteria from light mauve modelling marzipan. Shape a small cone over the end of a cocktail stick (toothpick). Apply a light coating of coconut oil, then use a no. 2 piping tube (tip) to mark small circles all over the paste.

Mould the leaves by rolling together two different tones of green marzipan into a small teardrop shape. Cut down the middle of each with the veining end of a dresden tool, then mark veins on each half to make two leaves. Roll thin strips of brown paste for the stem of the plant and secure it

▼ *Making wisteria.*

to the rails of the balustrade. The marzipan should stick to itself without sugar glue or egg white.

Attach the leaves and wisteria flowers to the plant. Repeat until you have covered the balustrade with wisteria.

Flowers in Pots

Make a small cone of green marzipan and hollow out the middle. Place in the flower container and indent it with a dresden tool. Roll small balls of coloured marzipan and hollow out the centre of each with a cocktail stick. Push into the green marzipan. Repeat until you

have sufficient to fill the flower container. Attach the flower containers to the top of the rails with sugar glue or egg white.

The Figurine

Position the figurine in the cut out oval section on the board.

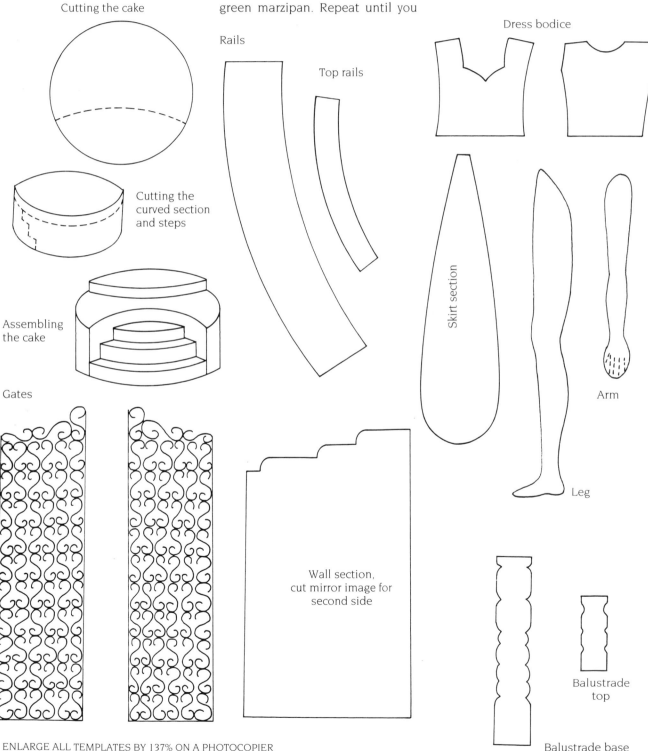

Cutting the cake

Cutting the curved section and steps

Assembling the cake

Gates

Rails

Top rails

Wall section, cut mirror image for second side

Dress bodice

Skirt section

Arm

Leg

Balustrade top

Balustrade base

ENLARGE ALL TEMPLATES BY 137% ON A PHOTOCOPIER

Flower Holder

This delicate flower holder makes a beautiful cake top decoration for a wedding, anniversary or special birthday. It may be filled with flowers made from sugar or silk. Simple flat modelling techniques are used, making this an ideal project for beginners who are just discovering the many uses of pastillage.

INGREDIENTS

155g (5 oz) Pastillage 1 or 2 see
    page 8
1.25kg (2½ lb) Royal Icing, see
    page 9
pink powder food colouring
20cm (8 in) round cake
Apricot Glaze, see page 14
750g (1½ lb) marzipan (almond
    paste)

EQUIPMENT

30cm (12 in) round cake board
13cm (5 in) oval cutter
8cm (3½ in) round cutter
large and medium rose petal cutters
drying board
corrugated drying sheet
silk or sugar flowers

The flower holder is shown on a cake with royal icing decorations. Notes on the cake decoration are included but the flower holder may be used as a top piece for any suitable cake design.

Flower Holder

Pastillage dries quickly, so use only the amount required for the sections being modelled. Use a porous drying board to absorb the moisture from the pastillage. Turn the pieces regularly during drying, otherwise the pastillage warps.

Shaping the Oval

Roll 125g (4 oz) pastillage into a cylinder shape, then roll it into rectangle just over 1mm (¹⁄₁₆ in) thick and 30cm (12 in) long. Cut a 5mm (¼ in) wide strip with a sharp kitchen knife. Place the oval

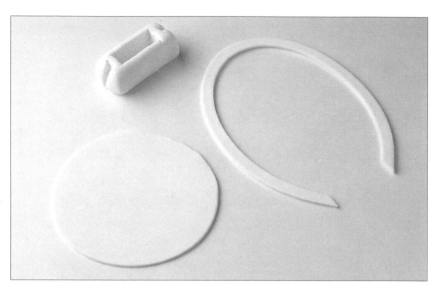

cutter on a drying board, then carefully lay the strip of paste around the outside of it. Cut the paste so that the ends fit the width of the flower stay, see template on page 70.

Base

Re-roll the pastillage to the same thickness and cut out an 8cm (3½ in) circle. Place on the drying board.

▲ *Base, handle and flower stay.*

Flower Stay

Roll a cylinder of pastillage, flatten the ends and cut out the centre with a scalpel, using the template on page 70 as a guide, indenting the ends so that the handle may be attached.

▼ *Petal sides for the flower holder, see page 70.*

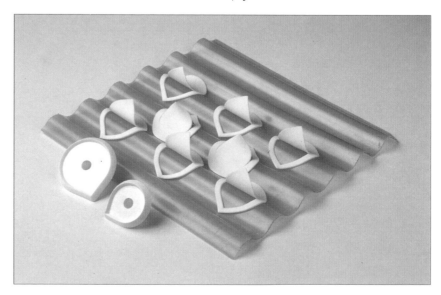

Petal Sides

Roll the pastillage thinly, then stamp out six petal shapes using the large rose cutter. Position the medium cutter inside one cut petal then apply pressure to the front and side of the cutting edge so that it cuts through three-quarters of the paste. Place the petal on the corrugated drying sheet and lift the centre of the petal so that it dries in an upwards curve. Repeat with the remaining petals. It is a good idea to make a few spare petals in case of breakages. Leave to dry for 24 hours.

Assembling the Sections

Carefully remove any rough edges on all pieces with a fine emery board. Dust the underneath of the curved sections of the petals with pink powder food colouring.

Place a small piece of sugarpaste in the flower stay, then secure it in the centre of the pastillage circle. Carefully position the oval handle in the ends of the flower holder and secure with white royal icing. Brush away excess icing with a damp paintbrush. Adjust the position of the handle to ensure that it is straight and upright, and check the position from the side as well as the front.

Attach the petal sections around the base with white royal icing. Allow the sections to dry for 2 – 3 hours before inserting flowers into the sugarpaste in the stay. Use

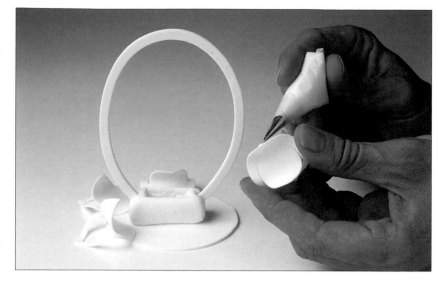

▲ *Attaching the petal sides to the flower holder.*

tweezers to avoid breaking the holder. Making a small hook in the end of the wire from the flowers will prevent them from falling over or twisting. Pipe white royal icing around each flower wire when it is positioned in the paste. This secures and also neatens the arrangement.

When positioning the flower holder on the cake, lift it by holding both sides of the oval.

The Decoration on the Cake

Brush the cake with apricot glaze and cover it with marzipan ready for applying royal icing, see page 14. Leave to dry for 3 – 5 days before coating with royal icing, see page 15. Cover the board with royal icing and leave to dry. Position the cake on the board when both are dry.

The side of the cake is decorated with piped scallops and flowers and the bottom edge is neatened with beading. The collar shape is echoed on the board, where 3-2-1 piping is added in pink, yellow and white.

The collar, see page 137, is runout in royal icing and decorated with small piped flowers and leaves, with curved lines following the edges. A line of white royal icing has been piped just inside the collar.

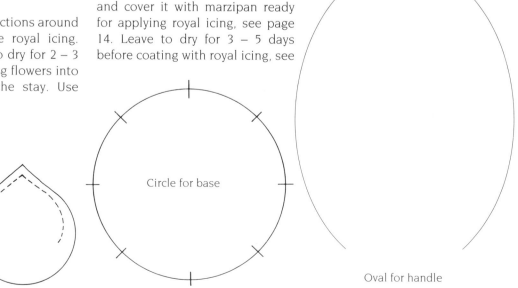

Flower stay

Petal section

ENLARGE ALL TEMPLATES BY 151% ON A PHOTOCOPIER

Circle for base

Oval for handle

Freestyle Modelling

Shape and form are the sources of inspiration for freestyle work which is a type of abstract modelling. Cut-out pastillage techniques are used here, with curved sections to create movement in the centrepiece which is linked by modelled marzipan flowers. The sections are repeated around the edge of this cake to give an elaborate finish.

INGREDIENTS

20cm (8 in) petal-shaped cake
Apricot Glaze, see page 14
875g (1¾ lb) marzipan (almond paste)
750g (1½ lb) Royal Icing, see page 9
375g (12 oz) sugarpaste
250g (8 oz) Pastillage 1, see page 8
125g (4 oz) Modelling Marzipan, see page 9

EQUIPMENT

28cm (11 in) cake board
drying board
5cm (2 in) round cutter
runout film
no. 1 piping tube (tip)
a few short lengths of spaghetti
umbrella tool
veining tool
masking tape

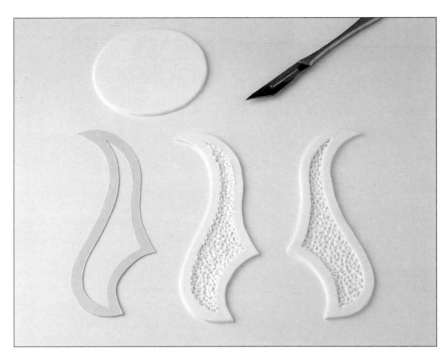

Freestyle Sections

▲ *The base and freestyle sections with template.*

Brush the cake with apricot glaze and cover it with marzipan, see page 14, ready for applying royal icing. Leave to dry for 3 – 5 days, then coat with white royal icing, see page 15. Cover the board with sugarpaste and leave to dry. Position the cake on the board.

Trace the side design template on page 73 and scribe it on the side of the cake. Use a no. 1 piping tube (tip) and white, mauve and lime green royal icing to pipe the design.

Make the cut out sections for the freestyle model and for decorating the edge of the cake. When dry, secure sections to the cake edge with soft royal icing.

Trace the template for the freestyle section, see page 73, transfer to thin card and cut out. Roll out the pastillage to 2mm (scant ⅛ in) thick, then use the template to cut out seven sections. Cut out the middle of each piece first, then cut around the outside of the template still in position. Transfer the sections to a drying board as they are cut; lay the card template over each piece to check that moving it has not distorted the shape. Turn the template over and cut another section in mirror image for the top.

Use a 5cm (2 in) round cutter to stamp out the pastillage base and transfer to the drying board. Leave all the sections until dry.

Use a fine emery board to remove any rough edges on the pieces. Lay the cut-out sections on runout film and secure with masking tape. Use a no. 1 piping

tube (tip) and white royal icing to pipe the filigree pattern in each section; dry.

Hyacinth

Colour 60g (2 oz) modelling marzipan deep mauve, then form a cone of marzipan on a short piece of spaghetti. Shape very small cones

from small pieces of marzipan. Place one small cone at the top and six around it. Continue to add more rows of cones until you have five to six rows. Push the piece of spaghetti into a soft piece of marzipan and leave to dry. Make four hyacinth flowers.

Daffodil

Colour 60g (2 oz) marzipan yellow and a small piece orange. Form a cone for the centre using a plastic modelling tool. Use a small pair of scissors to make two cuts on opposite sides of the cone, then cut each section twice more to give six petals. Dampen the blades of the scissors so that they cut the marzipan cleanly. Pinch the points of each petal together. Pinch the top and bottom of each petal to thin and flatten the paste slightly. Rock an umbrella tool gently on each petal to complete the shape.

Model a small piece of orange marzipan into a cone for the centre. Place this on the end of the umbrella tool and push it into the centre of the flower. Trim the surplus paste from the base of the flower, then allow to set.

Make five daffodils for the base of the arrangement, then model seven smaller ones for the top.

Leaves

The three different types of leaves are made by thinning the edges of small pieces of paste between polythene. If cutters are used, the marzipan must be rolled thinly otherwise the leaves will not retain their shape unless they are supported on crumpled cling film (plastic wrap), so that they set in the shapes of the indents. By shaping the leaves between plastic instead of using cutters, the edges can be worked quite thin, keeping the thickness in the middle of the leaf for support. This method also keeps the shine on the surface.

Rose Leaf

Roll a teardrop piece of green marzipan and place it between polythene, then apply pressure to the outer edges to shape and thin them. Use a veining tool to mark the veins through the polythene. Lift off the plastic and gently squeeze the paste on the back of the leaf, down the central vein. Make six rose leaves.

Ivy Leaf

Make five small teardrop shapes using two-tone green and cream marzipan in graduating sizes. Place the largest in the centre, then place two smaller pieces on either side. Cover with polythene, then smooth over the whole leaf to join the pieces together. Thin the edges and mark the veins through the polythene. Make six ivy leaves.

Daffodil Leaf

Roll a strand of marzipan, place it between polythene and thin the edges with one finger. Mark down the centre with the veining tool, then lift the polythene and gently twist the top part of the leaf to shape it. Make six daffodil leaves.

Assembling the Freestyle Model

Secure the flowers on a cone of sugarpaste with royal icing, checking that the arrangement is not too tall to go between the two curved sections.

Lay the mirror-image curved section and one other on runout film and join them together with royal icing. Allow to dry. Place the sections over the cone of flowers, securing the arrangement to the round base with royal icing. Support the two sections with small pieces of foam sponge and leave to dry for 12 hours. Place the model on the cake.

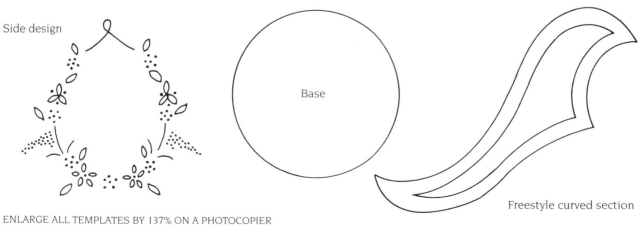

Side design

Base

Freestyle curved section

ENLARGE ALL TEMPLATES BY 137% ON A PHOTOCOPIER

Christening Crib

The classic crib and teddy decorations on this cake can be made in pink or blue for a girl or boy, or any other pastel colour as required. The teddy bear is also a useful model which can be made larger and used as a main decoration for other occasions, and for teddy-lovers of all ages!

INGREDIENTS

30cm (8in) oval cake
Apricot Glaze, see page 14
750g (1½ lb) marzipan (almond paste)
clear alcohol (vodka or gin)
1.1kg (2¼ lb) sugarpaste
125g (4oz) Pastillage 1 or 2, see page 8
small amount of Royal Icing, see page 9
90g (3 oz) Flower Paste, see page 8
selection of food colourings
Sugar Glue, see page 9
30g (1 oz) Modelling Paste, see page 8

EQUIPMENT

thin card
5cm (2 in) round cutter
straight edge frill cutter
cocktail stick (toothpick)
no. 1 piping tube (tip)
small round plunger cutter
small tracing wheel
paintbrushes
ball tool
tapered wooden dowel
dresden tool
blue baby ribbon to trim cake
blue ribbon to trim board

Brush the cake with apricot glaze and cover with marzipan, see page 14. Leave to dry. Colour 675g (1½ lb) sugarpaste blue. Brush the cake with clear alcohol, then cover with sugarpaste, see page 14. Cover the board with white sugarpaste and leave to dry before positioning the cake on it.

Cut a band of paper to fit around the cake. Divide it into 2cm (⅞ in) sections. Draw a line 5cm (2 in) up from the base of the template. Place around the cake and mark the points where the sections meet the line. Using soft royal icing and a no. 1 piping tube (tip), pipe a centre dot on each mark. Pipe dots around the base of the cake below the centre dots. Pipe lines of dots at an angle between the marker dots all around the cake. Add two dots between each section, from the marker dots and at the opposite angle, as shown on the cake.

Knead 30g (1 oz) each of white flower paste and sugarpaste together and use to make a boxed frill as for the crib side. Attach the

▼ *Making the crib.*

Proportions for teddy
(shown full size)

Oval for
cardboard template
to shape crib side

Curve template for drying
canopy support

ENLARGE BOTH TEMPLATES
BY 137% ON A PHOTOCOPIER

frill around the base of the cake with sugar glue and trim the base of the cake with ribbon. Make the cradle, teddy and building blocks and arrange them on the cake as shown, securing with sugar glue. Trim the board edge with ribbon.

Crib

Using the template on page 74, curve a strip of card into an oval, using the cutter to make sure the curved ends are neatly shaped. Secure with adhesive tape. Cut a strip of white cartridge paper to fit around the outside of the oval. Roll out the pastillage to 2mm (scant ⅛ in) thick. Cut a 4cm (1¾ in) wide strip long enough to fit around the card oval. Trim the edges of the paste so that they fit together neatly without overlapping. Secure the strip of paper around the outside to hold the pastillage in place and keep it in shape until it is dry. When the pastillage is dry, secure and neaten the join with royal icing.

Mix 30g (1 oz) flower paste with an equal quantity of sugarpaste, then colour blue. Roll out the paste thinly and cut out with a straight edge frill cutter. Use a cocktail stick (toothpick) to frill the edge of the paste slightly, rolling the stick gently from side to side with one finger on the edge of the paste. Use the end of a no. 1 piping tube (tip) to cut out the lace pattern around the edge of the

▲ *Making the head and pillow.*

diluted brown food colouring and mouth with skin tone. Secure the canopy support under the pillow with soft royal icing. Secure the pillow and baby in the crib.

Quilt

Roll out a thin rectangle of white flower paste twice the size needed to cover the baby. Mark squares on one half of the paste with the edge of a ruler. Turn the paste over and brush it with a little water. Using a no. 1 piping tube (tip), pipe beads of royal icing into the centres of the squares. Fold the unmarked side of the paste over the top. Turn the doubled paste over. Mark the squares again with a ruler and a tracing wheel to emphasize the quilting effect. Trim the edges.

Place the quilt over the baby, lifting the fold on one corner.

frilled paste. Fold the paste into box pleats, then secure it around the crib side with sugar glue. Make further pieces of frill as necessary to completely cover the side of the crib.

Canopy Support

Trace the canopy curve template on page 74. Re-roll the pastillage trimmings and cut out a strip measuring 11cm (4½ in) long by 8mm (⅓ in) wide. Shape the strip on its side following the drawn curve and leave to dry.

Crib Lining and Top Frill

Trace the oval template for the lining, see page 136. Roll out the flowerpaste thinly and cut out using the template. Frill the edge of the paste and cut a pattern with the piping tube (tip) point as for the box-pleated frill. Drape the paste over the crib side, gently easing it into the middle to form the lining for the crib. Adjust the edges of the paste so that they overhang the side evenly. Re-roll the paste trimmings and make a narrow frill as before to trim the edge of the crib. Allow to dry for 12 hours. Place the canopy support at the back of the crib.

▲ *The crib with lining and frill.*

Baby and Pillow

Roll a small ball of modelling paste for the baby's head. Use a small round plunger cutter to mark the mouth and eyes. Shape a cone of modelling paste for the body and place it in the crib to dry. Knead a small piece of sugarpaste with an equal piece of pastillage and shape it into a pillow. Indent the shape of the baby's head in the pillow and mark the edge with a small tracing wheel. Place the head on the pillow and position in the crib to dry.

When dry, paint on the hair with

▼ *Making the quilt.*

Leave to dry, then paint alternate sections blue. Secure to the baby with sugar glue.

Completing the Crib

For the canopy drape, roll out the remaining flower paste thinly and use the 5cm (2 in) round cutter or template on page 136 to cut out a circle. Cut the circle in half and roll the ball tool gently on the straight edge of each piece. Use a tapered wooden dowel to mark the lines on the paste. Use a dresden tool to mark between each line. Moisten the rounded edges and attach to the canopy support. Cut a strip of thinly rolled flower paste to neaten

the join between the drapes. Frill one edge, then cut the strip to length and frill the other edge. Attach the paste to the curved canopy support to neaten the drape. Colour a piece of flower paste blue and make three small bows to trim the drape.

Teddy

Colour the modelling paste pale brown. Roll a small ball of paste for the head and gently ease out two small sections for ears. Indent the ears with a dresden tool. Shape a small piece of paste for the snout and attach it to the face. Use a

veining tool to mark the eyes and a scalpel to mark the mouth.

Now roll a small cylinder of modelling paste for the body and secure it to the head. By inserting a cocktail stick (toothpick) into the base of the bear you will be able to hold the paste and model it more easily. Roll small cylinders for arms and legs, and attach them to the body. Then leave to dry.

Paint the eyes and nose with brown food colouring. Colour a little soft royal icing pale brown and pipe small areas of it on the bear. Stipple the icing with a brush to cover the bear and give a furry effect except on the base. If the base is covered, the bear will not sit straight.

Roll out a piece of blue flower paste and cut out a thin strip. Fold two loops in the middle of the bow, take the ends of the strip out and repeat to make a double bow, securing the ends in the centre with sugar glue. Leave the ends of the paste as ribbon tails. Cut a small section of paste and secure it around the middle of the bow with the join at the back.

Building Bricks

Roll a cylinder of modelling paste and flatten it between a ruler and palette knife. Cut it into small cubes and neaten them with a palette knife. Leave to dry, then paint on letters in different colours.

Gardening

This is the ideal cake for gardening enthusiasts, especially men, who are often difficult when it comes to selecting a suitable theme for a celebration cake. The gardener is modelled from marzipan, with spaghetti to help support the figure. The wheelbarrow and gardening tools are all modelled from pastillage but they can be made from marzipan if preferred, see page 9 on the choice of marzipan modelling paste. If the cake is intended for a flower gardener, model flowers following the instructions for the Freestyle Modelling cake, page 71, to replace the cabbages and leeks.

INGREDIENTS

20cm (8 in) petal cake
Apricot Glaze, see page 14
875g (1¾ lb) marzipan (almond paste)
clear alcohol (vodka or gin)
1.3kg (2¾ lb) sugarpaste
250g (8 oz) Modelling Marzipan, see page 9
125g (4 oz) Pastillage 1, see page 8
2 pieces of spaghetti

EQUIPMENT

30cm (12 in) petal cake board
wire brush
no. 1 piping tube (tip)
pieces of foam sponge
cocktail sticks (toothpicks)
small rose petal cutter
kitchen foil
2 dresden tools
piece of styrofoam or polystyrene
2 cake dowels
paintbrush

Make the wheelbarrow and the small garden box before the figure for decorating this cake, as the box is used to support the gardener's leg.

Brush the cake with apricot glaze and cover it with marzipan, see page 14. Colour 500g (1 lb) sugarpaste green and roll out a piece large enough to cover the top of the cake. Brush just the top of the cake with alcohol. Cover the top of the cake with the rolled green sugarpaste, trimming off excess

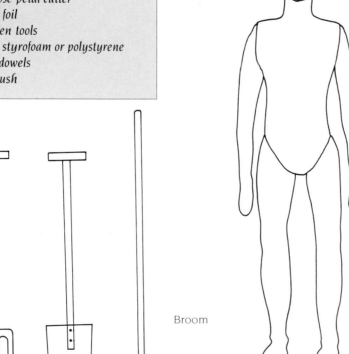

ENLARGE ALL TEMPLATES BY 137% ON A PHOTOCOPIER

Fork   Spade   Broom

Diagram of figure for proportions

and smoothing down the edges thinly and evenly. Using the cake board as a guide, cut a petal template, fold it in half and cut off 2.5cm (1 in) all around the edge. Cover the board with green sugarpaste. Open the template out and place on the board, then mark the edge of the template on the sugarpaste. Leave to dry.

Cut a template slightly smaller than the top of the cake, using the baking tin as a guide. Colour 675g (1½ lb) sugarpaste blue. Place the template on top of the cake. Brush the side and the top edge of the cake up to the template with alcohol. Remove the template and cover the cake with the blue sugarpaste. Replace the template and cut right through the blue sugarpaste, then lift off the top so that the green paste shows.

Stipple the green paste with a wire brush, then colour with dark green food colouring. Use the template from the top of the cake to make a template for a section of garden to fit in one curve of the lawn. Cut it out in rolled-out brown sugarpaste. Dampen it with alcohol and place on the cake, then texture the surface to look like soil and indent the furrows. Cover the board with green sugarpaste. Place the cake on the board. Cut a strip of rolled-out, brown sugarpaste and place this around the base of the cake, on the board. Smooth the join and texture the paste to look like soil. Using green royal icing and a no. 1 piping tube (tip), pipe grass edges around the base of the cake and around the cabbage plot on the cake top.

▲ *Making the wheelbarrow.*

Follow the instructions for making the balustrade on A Walk in the Park cake, see page 66, for making the fence posts. Cut narrow strips of pastillage for the top of the fence. Secure the fence posts and strips to the side of the cake with matching royal icing.

Use a no. 1 piping tube (tip) and matching royal icing to pipe the trellis and neaten the top of the fence with a line of icing.

Position the gardener on the cake, securing the feet with softened marzipan and sugar glue. Support for 12 hours until firmly set. Then insert the garden fork into the gardener's hand and secure the wheelbarrow to the cake with royal icing. Arrange the other tools on the cake.

Wheelbarrow and Garden Box

Colour the pastillage brown, leaving it marbled with colour. Using the templates on page 136, cut out all the sections for the wheelbarrow and box, and leave them to dry for 24 hours, turning regularly. Smooth down any rough edges with a fine emery board. Dust the surface with light brown powder food colouring.

Join the front and side panels of the wheelbarrow with soft royal icing. Remove any surplus icing with a damp paintbrush. Support the pastillage with pieces of foam sponge until the icing has set. Repeat for the opposite side and then the end panel. Allow to set.

Turn the wheelbarrow over and secure the wheel in place with royal icing. Leave to dry. Fix the handles and legs to the wide end of the wheelbarrow.

Garden Tools

Spade

Roll a small rectangle of pastillage, then cut out the spade shape using the template on page 78. Roll a thin cylinder for the handle, cutting it to the length required to fit the figure. Cut a shorter handle for the top of the spade. Dry on a piece of foam sponge. Assemble with royal icing when completely dry, then brush with powder food colouring.

Fork

Roll a rectangle of pastillage for the fork then cut the prongs with a sharp scalpel, see template on page 78. Make a handle as for the spade. Leave to dry before assembling.

Garden Broom

Roll the handle as for the spade, then cut the base for the broom using the template on page 78. Make a small hole in the base for the handle. Leave the pieces to dry before assembling with royal icing. Make a base for the bristles; use a

▼ *Cabbages and leeks, opposite, with garden tools.*

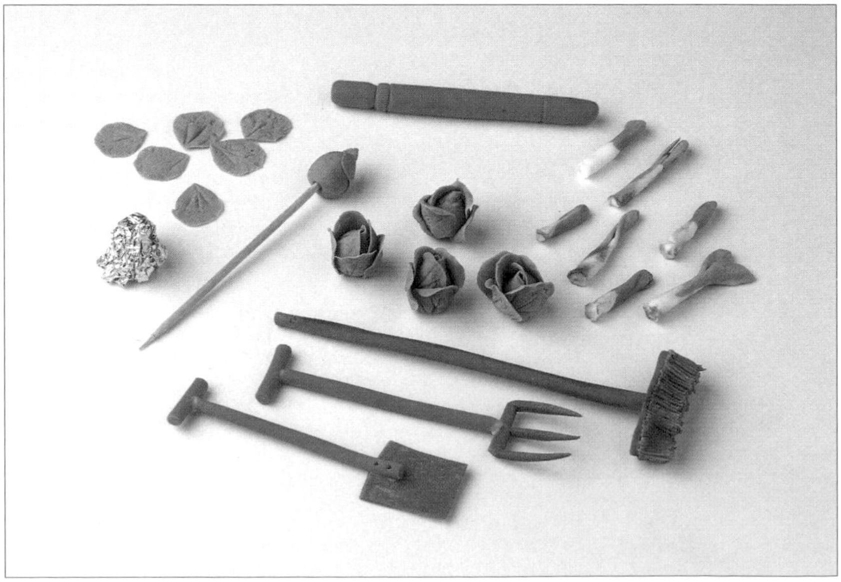

no. 1 piping tube (tip) to pipe a line of royal icing down the centre of the broom base. Repeat until the icing is 1cm (½ in) deep. Allow to set. When the icing is dry, pipe over it, back and forth to form the bristles. When dry, dust with powder colouring.

Cabbages and Leeks

Cabbages

Roll a piece of green flower paste into a small cone, then insert a cocktail stick (toothpick) into the base. Roll out the paste and stamp out seven small rose petals using the cutter – the paste must not be too thin. Crumple a small piece of kitchen foil, then use it to emboss the petals so that they look like cabbage leaves. Add a few veins with a dresden tool. Fix the leaves to the cone with sugar glue, overlapping them and making cabbages of different sizes by adding more leaves. Remove the cabbages from the cocktail sticks when dry.

Leeks

Blend a small piece each of white and green flower paste together, with the white at one end. Roll into a cylinder, then make a short cut into the green paste; make another short cut into one side of the green paste and flatten all three sections using the dresden tool to shape the leek. Pinch the edges of the white paste with a small pair of tweezers to form the roots. Dust with brown powder food colouring.

The Gardener

Use the proportions of the body for the gardener on page 78 as a guide when modelling the character. Study a human face before you start, as this will give

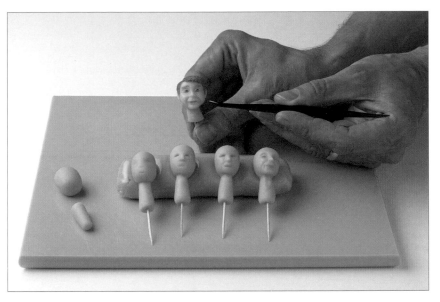

▲ *Stages in making the head.*

you a good idea of the proportions for features.

Head

Colour the modelling marzipan for the gardener, using about 125g (4 oz) for the body. I used a little chestnut brown food colouring to give the skintone colour. Colour the remaining marzipan for the trousers and shoes, grey and brown as shown or in the colour of your choice, leaving some paste uncoloured for the shirt.

Roll a small ball of marzipan for the head and shape it into an oval. Form the neck from a small cylinder, then insert a cocktail stick (toothpick) and attach the neck to the head. Smooth the join. Wrap a spare piece of marzipan in cling film (plastic wrap) and make an indent in it to support the head; place the head in this while modelling the face.

Mark the indents for the eyes using a dresden tool, then add a small piece of marzipan for the nose. Indent the eyes, adding small pieces for the white and pushing them into the eye shape with the dresden tool. If you want the figure to have chubby cheeks, add small pieces of marzipan and smooth them in well. Mark the

shape for the mouth, then roll very small pieces of pink-brown marzipan and place them over the mouth for lips. Indent the lips and shape the mouth into a smile or grin. Roll small pieces of marzipan for the eyelids to part-cover the eye. Make the eyeball from darker brown marzipan, then position it in the direction in which you want the figure to look. Add the eyebrows, then allow the head to set for 12 hours in an airtight container.

Model the ears from small ovals of marzipan, see diagram on page 78, and attach them to the head, placing their tops at eye level. Roll small pieces of marzipan for the hair, attach them to the head in the required hair style. Texture the marzipan as shown on page 29, for the Animal Caricatures.

Body

Shape the marzipan for the body parts following the templates. Hollow out the top where the neck is to be inserted. Remove the cocktail stick (toothpick) from the head and insert a piece of spaghetti. Attach the head and neck to the body.

Form the arm sockets and shape the chest and waist. The lower part of the body should be shaped

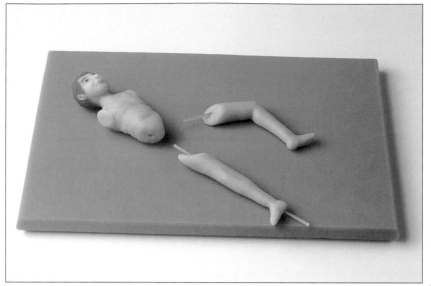

▲ *The legs and body for the gardener.*

▲ *Supporting the gardener in his pose until dry.*

with hollows for the legs to be added.

Roll out the marzipan between two sheets of polythene for the shirt and trousers, see page 25, then allow to rest for a few minutes before cutting out a piece large enough to wrap around the figure. Gather the marzipan around the neck, then make a cut and model the open neck for the front of the shirt. Fold back the top corners of the shirt to form the collar.

Mark the waist so that the shirt appears to be tucked into the trousers. To prevent the shirt from being flattened at the back, insert a cocktail stick (toothpick) in the base of the gardener and push it into styrofoam to set.

Legs

Roll a cylinder for the legs, then cut it in half. Shape the legs and insert a length of spaghetti into each from the foot end, pushing it out at the top of the leg. Leave 1cm (½ in) protruding from the top of the leg.

To model the leg which is bent, hold the body and place the garden box under the leg, then adjust the angle at the knee bend and at the top of the leg, where it joins the body. Leave the legs to set for 12 hours.

The shoes are made as for the Animal Caricatures, see page 35. Cover the legs with the rolled-out marzipan. Cut a strip of the marzipan for the trouser waist band, placing the join at the front. Shape the paste around the leg socket. Make a small hole in the body and brush sugar glue around it. Insert the end of spaghetti supporting the leg and smooth the join. Position the other leg, then support the standing figure with the cake dowels pushed into styrofoam. Roll a cylinder of marzipan, wrap it in cling film (plastic wrap) and position it under the bent leg. Position the small box under the foot, then allow the figure to set, covered with a plastic bag

Arms

Roll a cylinder of marzipan. Make one end into an oval shape to resemble a hand. Make a 'V'-shaped cut for the thumb and three cuts for the fingers. Gently open out the fingers and roll them from side to side between the tips of your thumb and index finger.

Hollow the palm of the hand and shape the wrist. Mark the knuckles on the back of the hand, then model the joints on the fingers by using the widest ends of two dresden tools. Hold a tool in each hand as this will allow you to form

the shape of the fingers. Gently bend the fingers so that they are in position for holding the garden spade. Use a small paintbrush to form the shape, then remove it and allow the hand to set. Repeat for the other hand, shaping the fingers to fit over the leg of the figure.

Cover the arms with thinly rolled marzipan, gathering it around the upper part to resemble rolled-up sleeves. Secure the arms on the figure with a little sugar glue. Neaten the sleeve joints, blending the edges of marzipan together. Support the arms with short lengths of cake dowel until set.

Cat in the Window

A small container is used as a base on which to model the cat in this window. If a solid block of pastillage is used, as it dries out it is likely to expand and crack. By using a container as the base, the pastillage dries more quickly and evenly, and small pieces of pastillage can be added to define the shape without causing drying problems.

INGREDIENTS

20 x 15cm (8 x 6 in) oval cake
Apricot Glaze, see page 14
1 kg (2 lb) marzipan (almond paste)
clear alcohol (vodka or gin)
1.25 kg (2½ lb) sugarpaste
selection of food colourings
small amount of Royal Icing, see
*   page 9*
125 g (4 oz) Pastillage 1 or 2, see
*   page 8*
60 g (2 oz) Modelling Paste, see
*   page 8*

EQUIPMENT

28 x 20cm (11 x 8 in) oval cake
*   board*
masking tape
airbrush
paintbrush
no. 0 and 2 x no. 1 piping tubes
(tips)
empty film container and lid or small
*   container, see method*
dresden tool
whitener (titanium oxide) or white
*   powder food colouring*
6 white stamens
marzipan hyacinth, see page 71
1m (1⅛ yd) of 5mm (¼ in) wide
*   ribbon*

Cut the cake following the diagram below. Slice horizontally through a third of the cake, 2.5cm (1 in) from the base. Then cut down through the cake to remove a semi-circular piece. Place the cut-out piece end down on top of the cake to create the curved top for the window. Trim the corners at the bottom of the curved piece so that it fits neatly on top of the cake. Use a little apricot glaze to keep the cake in place.

Brush the assembled cake with apricot glaze and cover with marzipan, see page 14. Allow to dry, then brush with alcohol and cover with sugarpaste, see page 14. Cover the board with sugarpaste. Leave to dry.

Lay strips of masking tape across the board and airbrush pink. Remove the masking tape to reveal the stripes. Leave to dry. Use a no. 0 piping tube (tip) and dark pink royal icing to pipe the stripes and dot flower design over the airbrushed stripes. Alternatively, these can be painted on using a fine paintbrush and concentrated colour.

Mark the window outline on the back of the cake, using the template on page 137. Use food colouring to paint the view from the window, leaving the frame uncoloured. Gradually build up the scene, allowing each stage to dry first before painting the next with another colour. Paint the frame and outline it with dark brown when dry, adding a cross where the sections of frame meet.

Paint the woodgrain effect on the flat section of cake in front of the window. Allow the brown to dry before painting on the grain of the wood in grey. Leave to dry.

Colour the remaining sugarpaste pale pink, roll it out and cut out two 25 x 20cm (10 x 8 in) oblongs for the curtains. Cut a third oblong measuring 7.5 x 18cm (7 x 3 in) for the drape at the top. Pipe the spot pattern onto the paste with soft royal icing. Drape the curtains on either side and around the back of the window, attaching them at the top with sugar glue. The curtains should meet around the back of the cake.

Cutting the cake

Fold the smaller oblong of sugar-paste into a swag, brush the top of the curtains with sugarpaste and attach the swag, draping the back neatly and ensuring that the front is pinched into shape.

Colour a small piece of modelling paste a darker shade of pink and cut out two 9 x 3.5cm (3½ x 1½ in) strips for tie backs. Brush the back of the tie backs with sugar glue, pull back the front of the curtains and fix the tie backs in place.

Position the cat and the pot of flowers in front of the window.

Cat

Dust the outside of an empty film container with cornflour (corn-starch). If you do not have a film container, you will need a similar object which will fit into the space indicated by the dotted line on the drawing of the cat on page 137.

▼ *Modelling the head.*

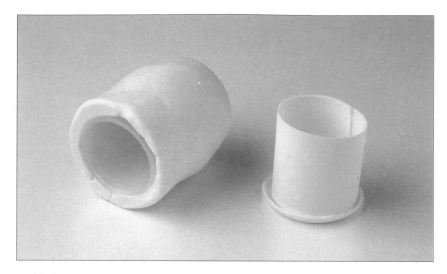

▲ *The hollow body for the cat.*

Mould about 60g (2 oz) pastillage over the container. Remove the container occasionally to make sure that the paste does not stick to it. Leave to dry for 12 hours.

Head

Use the outline of a cat on page 137 as a guide to proportions and shape. Roll a ball of pastillage for the head. Use the line drawing for the basic shape of the cat as a guide to proportions and shape.

Pinch two pieces of paste out to form the ears then use the dresden tool to shape them. Model the eyes, nose and mouth shape. Make a small hole in the base of the head, then leave to dry for 12 hours.

Body

Remove the film case from the base of the cat. Roll a small ball of paste for the shoulders, blend it onto the body, shaping the shoulders as you smooth the paste in position. Use a scalpel to cut the sides at an angle where the back and front legs are to be attached. Trim a little paste from under the back part of the body to give the cat a rounded shape. Do not cut into the pastillage too deeply. Roll two small cylinders of pastillage for the front legs and attach them, blending the join well. Make two small chicken-drumstick shapes for the back legs, flatten them and attach them at the side of the body, curving the front of the paws and smoothing the joins well.

▼ *Attaching the paws to the cat.*

Completing the Cat

Position the head on the body. Roll a strip of paste for a tail and attach it at the back. Then adjust the shape of the cat to the required position and amend the features, if required, to make a plump animal. Leave the paste to dry before painting the features.

Mix food colouring to a thick consistency with white powder food colouring or whitener powder. Paint the eyes first. Prepare two piping bags fitted with no. 1 piping tubes (tips), one filled with white royal icing and the other filled with an orange-brown colour. Pipe small areas of royal icing over the cat and brush it with a paintbrush to create the fur effect. Pipe icing around the eyes so that they appear deeply set.

Attach three small pieces of white stamen to each side of the head for the whiskers, then leave to dry. Brush the fur with powder food colouring when dry.

Pot Plant

The small plant pot is made using the film case, with the lid for the saucer. Cover the pot with pastillage and dry. Paint a pattern on the side of the pot, then fill with pastillage. Place a piece of dark brown sugarpaste on top and texture the surface to represent soil, see page 71. Place the hyacinth in the pot. Use paste trimmings to model tiny flowers and leaves.

Welcome Home

This unusual top decoration is ideal for a cake intended to welcome someone home from travels, hospital or a long stay in a foreign country. It is also a good theme for a 'welcome to your new home' cake. The table is left uncovered so that the construction is easily seen but it can be draped with a decorative cloth.

INGREDIENTS

20cm (8 in) round cake
Apricot Glaze, see page 14
750g (1½ lb) marzipan (almond paste)
625g (1¼ lb) sugarpaste
500g (1 lb) Royal Icing, see page 9
185g (6 oz) Pastillage 1 or 2, see page 8
small amount of Flower Paste, see page 8
60g (2 oz) Modelling Paste, see page 8

EQUIPMENT

30cm (12 in) round cake board
no. 1 and 2 piping tubes (tips)
small chisel paintbrush
diamond aspic cutter
1cm (½ in), 1.5cm (¾ in), 2cm (⅞ in), 3.5cm (1½ in), 5cm (2 in) and 8cm (3¼ in) round cutters
cardboard roll from kitchen paper
fine emery board
tracing wheel
70cm (¾ yd) each of pale green and pale pink 3mm (⅛ in) ribbon for cake
1m (1⅛ yd) pale green 1cm (½ in) ribbon for board edge

Brush the cake with apricot glaze and cover with marzipan for applying royal icing, see page 14, and leave to dry. Apply three coats of royal icing, see page 15, and leave to dry. Coat the board with royal icing and leave to dry. Place the cake on the board. Trim the bottom of the cake with narrow pink and green ribbon.

Colour a third of the sugarpaste pink and cover the top of the cake. Colour the remaining sugarpaste green. Cut out a 15cm (6 in) circular template. Roll out the green sugarpaste. Brush just the top edge of the cake with alcohol and cover with the green sugarpaste. Use the template to cut a circle from the middle of the paste and lift it off so that the pink paste shows. Trim the paste allowing 4cm (1¾ in) to drape down the side of the cake.

Using a no. 1 piping tube (tip) and white royal icing, pipe a picot edge around the green paste, to resemble a tablecloth. Pipe the pattern of dots around the top and bottom edges of the green paste. Pipe the bead border around the bottom of the cake.

Make the table and chair and secure them to the top of the cake. Trim the board with green ribbon.

Table

Colour a quarter of the pastillage light brown, another quarter dark brown, then roll and twist both pieces together to give a wood grain effect. Roll out to 2mm (scant ⅛ in) thick. Cut out the top, base, under-table support, legs and base disk. Leave on a drying board for 24 hours, turning occasionally.

Roll a cylinder of paste for the central leg and mark as for the balustrade, see page 66, then leave to dry on foam sponge. When dry, sand off any rough edges with a fine emery board and ensure that the top and bottom are level.

Mix light and dark brown powder food colouring and brush the table sections – a small chisel brush is best for the edge. Apply colour to the light streaks.

Mix a little pastillage with sugar glue to make a soft paste and use this to secure all the pieces together. Attach the base disk to the central leg, then secure two opposite legs. Attach the remaining two legs, adjusting them so that the table stands upright. Leave to dry for 24 hours.

Secure the table base support to the table top. Insert the central leg, then ensure that the top is level and the table stands well. Leave to dry for 12 hours.

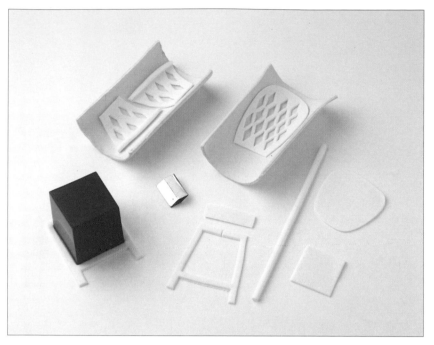

Chair

Cut a cardboard tube from a kitchen roll in half. Open out one half. Roll out the pastillage to 1.5mm (generous ⅟₁₆ in) thick. Cut out the back of the chair using the template on page 89. Use the diamond aspic cutter to cut out the sections, then place the chair back in the curved section of cardboard and leave to dry. Cut out the chair arms, then roll the widest ends slightly before placing in the other piece of tube to dry. Cut out the under and upper seat sections.

Roll out the pastillage to 1mm (scant ⅟₁₆ in) thick. Cut out the side frame for the chair. Use an empty container from cocktail sticks (toothpicks) to stamp out the middle section, if available, or cut the section with a scalpel. Cut the top of the chair frame and remove a very small piece of paste, then bring the strips together again and secure with sugar glue. By the time the section is removed, and the strips stuck back together, the top of the chair frame should be the same size as the under seat. Make a second frame for the other side of the chair.

Roll a thin cylinder of pastillage to 1.5mm (generous ⅟₁₆ in) in diameter and dry on foam sponge. Cut this to the exact size when dry to make cross bars between the legs at the front and back of the chair.

Assembling the Pieces

Use the pastillage and sugar glue paste, as for the table, when assembling the chair. Use a small strip of emery board to file the edges of the diamond sections in the back of the chair and smooth all other rough edges. Secure the under seat to the upper seat. Turn the seat over and secure the two side frames. Support with foam sponge until dry. Turn the chair upright, then measure the size for the cross bars and cut the cylinder to length. Attach the cross bars to the frame.

Secure the back of the chair to the seat and support it with foam sponge until dry. Secure the arms, again supporting them with foam sponge until dry. Leave the chair to dry for 12 hours.

Cushions

Colour half the modelling paste for the cushions: the picture shows one pink and one green cushion. Shape the paste to fit the chair seat and mark the buttons with a no. 2 piping tube (tip). Mark creases with the veining end of a dresden tool. Dry on foam sponge. Colour the second piece of paste and model the shell-shaped cushion. Mark the pattern with the dresden tool and a tracing wheel. Place in the chair to dry in shape.

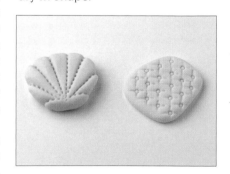

Vase, Flowers and Book

Colour a small piece of flower paste green for the flower stems and cut thin strands; allow to dry. Make the flowers following the instructions on page 67.

For the vase, roll a cone of modelling paste and shape it over a cone tool to hollow it out. Flatten the bottom and leave to dry. Paint the floral design on the side of the vase. Fill with flowers and secure to the table top.

Roll out the flower paste and cut a small rectangle for the book cover. Mark two lines for the spine of the book. Roll out and cut modelling paste for the pages, cut out four small rectangles to fit in the book, making them progressively smaller. Stick these on the paste with sugar glue, then fold the paste over to cover the book. Flatten the spine of the book slightly. Leave to dry. Paint a title on the book, as required, and secure the book to the table top.

ENLARGE ALL TEMPLATES BY 137% ON A PHOTOCOPIER

Table top: cut 2mm (scant ⅛ in) thick

Under table support: cut 2mm (scant ⅛ in) thick

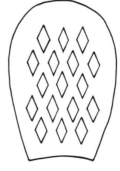

Vase   Book

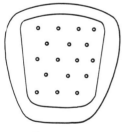

Upper seat

Chair side, cut 1mm (¹⁄₁₆ in) thick

Chair back: cut 1.5mm (generous ¹⁄₁₆ in) thick

Cushion

Table base disc

Arm: reverse for second side

Under seat

Table legs

Table plinth

Nature Reserve

INGREDIENTS

20cm (8 in) long hexagonal cake
Apricot Glaze, see page 14
750g (1½ lb) marzipan (almond
    paste)
1.6kg (3¾ lb) sugarpaste
selection of food colourings
clear alcohol (vodka or gin)
small amount of Royal Icing, see
    page 9
125g (4 oz) Pastillage 1 or 2, see
    page 8
cornflour (cornstarch)
90g (3 oz) Flower Paste, see page 8
sugar glue

EQUIPMENT

no. 1 piping tube (tip)
paintbrush
ball, cone, dresden and dog bone tools
single eyelet plunger cutter
1m (1⅛ yd) of 1cm (½ in) wide
    brown ribbon

Brush the cake with apricot glaze and cover it with marzipan. Leave to dry. Cut out a template for the cake top, see page 93. Set aside 220g (7 oz) white sugarpaste. Colour a third of the remainder pale blue, the rest a slightly darker blue. Brush the cake with alcohol. Cover with the darker blue paste. Place the template on top of the cake, mark the position for the pond and follow the instructions on page 40 for modelling the water.

Trace the templates for cutting the paste around the side of the cake and the top section. Cut a strip of paper to fit around the cake, then cut out the template shape in the edge of the paper. Roll out the pale blue paste to 3mm (⅛ in) thick and large enough to cover the cake. Brush the sugarpaste around the top edge of the cake with alcohol – do not brush the area for modelled water

in the middle, nor the sides of the cake. Cover with the paste and smooth to the shape of the cake. Fit the template around the cake sides and cut the top layer of paste with a scalpel. Place the second template on top of the cake and cut through the top layer of sugarpaste. Lift the sugarpaste off the middle of the cake, neaten the edge into the hollow. Colour the water blue and green for depth and contrast. Brush soft white royal icing in small areas to resemble wave peaks. Texture the paste so that the duck will fit on top. Leave to dry.

Mix the remaining blue sugarpaste with 125g (4 oz) of the reserved white sugarpaste, leaving them part-mixed to give a marbled effect. Cover the board with the marbled paste and leave to dry. Place the cake on the board.

Trace the designs for the cake sides, see page 93, and transfer to the cake. The design is applied by outlining the petals with blue royal icing, using a no. 1 piping tube (tip). Then use a damp paintbrush to brush the line of icing towards the middle of the flower, leaving a darker, slightly raised edge around each petal. Pipe the bead work

around the base of the cake. Pipe the stems and small leaves in green. Outline the edge of the scalloped paste.

Cut 50 to 60 reeds from green flower paste, see page 39, and allow to dry. Colour the reeds with green petal dust, then cut small holes in the sugarpaste and push the reeds into the cuts. Make small stones from sugarpaste, see page 39, and position them around the edges of the pond, securing with a little royal icing.

Duck

Work the pastillage until it is soft and pliable, then shape it into a cone using the top view template, see page 93, as a guide to base size. Hollow out the centre with your index finger, pinching the outside with your thumb. The hole should become smaller as you work down the length of the body. As you make the hole smaller, fold surplus paste back into the body. Place the hollowed paste into a small container filled with cornflour to dry. The cornflour supports

▼ *Shaping the duck's body.*

▲ *Cutting the feathers for the duck.*

page 92. Mark the feathers as before and secure to the back of the duck.

For the third row of feathers, roll the brown paste thinly. Use a single eyelet plunger cutter and cut out seven feathers for each side. Mark the centre of each with the dresden tool, then secure the feathers from tail towards the head, overlapping and with pointed-end facing the tail.

For the fourth row, re-roll the blue-grey paste thinly. Cut out the paste with the single eyelet cutter, mark the centre of each feather, then attach them in a semi-circle, overlapping towards the head of the duck.

the paste and keeps it in shape during drying.

Take a piece of pastillage about a third of the size of the body. Roll it into a ball then use a dog bone tool to hollow out the top for the head. Adjust the shape of the head, then form the eye sockets with the ball tool. Leave in cornflour to dry.

Combine five walnut-sized pieces of flower paste with five pea-sized pieces of sugarpaste. Colour the pieces blue-grey, beige, orange-red, black, and white. Brush the surplus cornflour from the duck base and the head, then secure the head to the body with softened pastillage mixed with sugar glue. Allow to dry until firm.

Mould the white paste over the breast, side and tail. Mark small lines on the paste with the veining end of the dresden tool.

Feathers

Use the beige paste for the under feathers. Roll out a piece of paste to fit over duck's back, smooth it in place, marking lines horizontally with the dresden tool to form the feathers. Make small cuts under each line with a scalpel, then mark the horizontal lines again.

Tail feathers

Roll the brown paste thinly, Using the template on page 92 as a guide, cut out the tail feathers with a scalpel. Mark small cuts down each side, then mark down the centre with the dresden tool. Overlap the tail feathers as you secure them to the body with sugar glue.

For the second row of tail feathers, mix the blue-grey paste with a small piece of the brown paste. Roll out, then cut to shape using template B as a guide, see

Wings

Roll 15g (½ oz) white flower paste, 2mm (scant ⅛ in) thick at one end (top edge of wing) and becoming very thin at the other end (bottom edge of wing). Place the wing template on the paste with the pointed end at the thickest end of the paste. Cut out and soften the cut edges between your thumb and index finger. Curve the wings against the duck, then support them with a small piece of foam sponge and leave to dry for 3 – 4 hours.

▼ *Attaching the wings.*

Head Features

For the beak, roll a small piece of red-orange paste into a cone. Lengthen it slightly, then cut it with a scalpel to form the top and lower beak. Mark nostrils on the beak side, then secure the beak to the head with sugar glue.

Secure a small sausage of black paste to the head, ensuring that it meets the beak. Use a scalpel and dresden tool to make small cuts along the black paste.

For eyes, mix a small speck of white paste with black paste, roll the paste into a ball and secure it in the eye socket.

Completing the Wings and Feathers

Secure the wings in place with flower paste mixed with a little sugar glue. Pipe over the wings with soft white royal icing using a no 1. piping tube (tip). Use a damp medium paintbrush to brush the icing down the wings in short strokes.

Dress feathers

Roll black and white paste to give a streaky effect. Cut the long, thin under-feathers with a scalpel and secure them to the side of the duck. Attach three or four layers.

Then roll out the orange-red paste thinly. Cut small, feathery sections and attach them, starting at the back of the neck and applying them all around as shown.

Roll out a piece each of black and white paste thinly, then place one on top of the other. Cut the long feathers for the top of the head and secure with sugar glue. Pipe white royal icing around over the edge of the orange feathers, then smooth down with a damp brush.

Final Detail

Brush dark brown powder food colouring down the beige base feathers and over the tail feathers. Brush black powder food colouring down the edges of the second row of feathers. Paint fine white lines down the centre of the blue-grey feathers. Lightly dust the wings with orange powder food colouring. Apply two coats of a clear confectioners' glaze or gum arabic to the eyes. Position the completed duck on the cake and trim the board edge with cake braid and ribbon.

▲ *Painting the final detail.*

MODELLING MEMO

To make a permanent keepsake of the top decoration, instead of fitting the water section into the cake, model it separately and allow to set completely, then place the duck in position. The separate plaque can then be fitted into the top of the cake and removed before the cake is cut. The top of the cake should be covered completely with blue sugarpaste before the outer paler coating is applied if the water is to be inserted as a separate plaque.

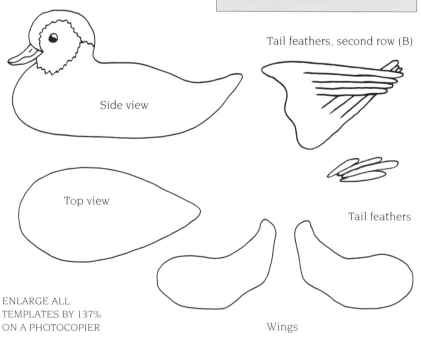

Side view

Top view

Tail feathers, second row (B)

Tail feathers

Wings

ENLARGE ALL
TEMPLATES BY 137%
ON A PHOTOCOPIER

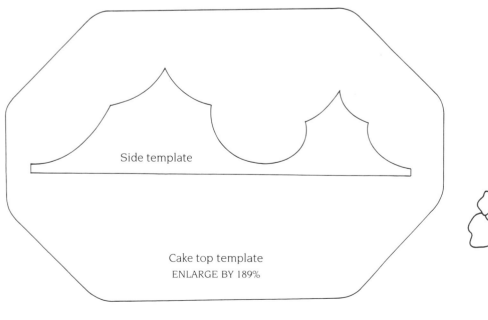

Side template

Cake top template
ENLARGE BY 189%

Side design
ENLARGE BY 137%

Christmas Eve

This cake captures the excitement of Christmas Eve, as the bustling rabbits busy themselves with the Christmas tree. Bas relief modelling techniques are accentuated on this cake by hollowing the top of the cake to make the background appear further away.

INGREDIENTS

23cm (9 in) oval cake
Apricot Glaze, see page 14
1.25kg (2¼ lb) marzipan (almond paste)
clear alcohol (vodka or gin)
1.25kg (2½ lb) sugarpaste
selection of food colourings
250g (8 oz) Modelling Paste, see page 8
60g (2 oz) Flower Paste, see page 8
small amount of Royal Icing, see page 9
silver sparkle petal dust

EQUIPMENT

30cm (12 in) oval cake board
no. 00, 1 and 0 piping tubes (tips)
24-gauge green wire
runout film
angled tweezers
clear plastic file
ball tool
3mm (⅛ in) wide red ribbon
1.2m (1¼ yd) of 1cm (½ in) red ribbon to trim board edge

Hollow out the top of the cake, down to a point in the middle, as shown on the template page 138. Brush with apricot glaze and cover with marzipan, see page 14. Colour the sugarpaste pale green. Brush the cake with alcohol and coat with sugarpaste, see page 14, then allow to dry for 3 – 4 days. Cover the board with sugarpaste and leave to dry. Place the cake on the board.

Background

Colour 90g (3 oz) modelling paste red and roll it out thinly. Cut the paste using the template on page

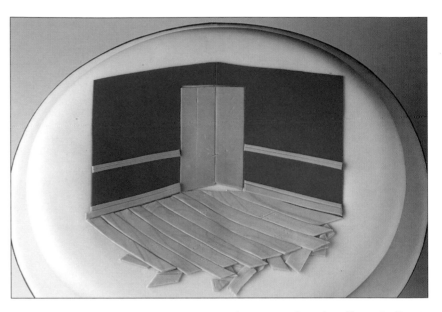

▲ *Applying the background.*

138, then place it in the hollow on the cake. Check that the paste corresponds to the cut shape of the cake and that it is in the correct position before you stick it down with sugar glue.

Colour 90g (3 oz) modelling paste a light brown and 30g (1 oz) dark brown, then roll together to

give a wood grain effect. Roll out and cut strips of paste for the floorboards. Place the floorboards on the cake, supporting their ends on small pieces of spare paste until dry. Cut the dado rail from strips of paste and dry these on the cake. Cut the skirting board and dry it on the cake.

▼ *Adding the dresser, see page 95.*

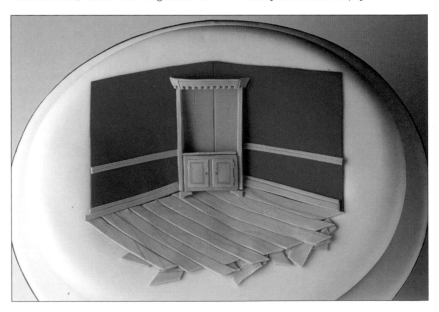

Dresser

Use the templates on page 96. Cut the background section for the dresser from rolled-out modelling paste. Then secure it on the background with a little sugar glue. Cut out the side sections and place on the back of the dresser so that they can dry to shape. Cut the cupboard section, then mark on the door with the spade end of a modelling tool.

Place a small piece of paste behind the cupboard, then place between the two upright sections to dry. Cut the feet, by using the wide end of a piping tube (tip) to cut a circle of paste, then trim the four edges to give the leg shape. Cut the top of the cupboard, the shelves and doors. Cut the cornice piece to fit around the top and side. Stick the front and side pieces of the cornice to the top of the dresser. Secure the uprights of the dresser to the back section, then add the top. Fit the legs with soft royal icing, then allow to dry. Fix the cupboard on to the back section, then add the top of the dresser. Add the shelves, filling any small gaps with soft royal icing.

Paint the panels on the doors and pipe small lines on each using a no. 1 piping tube (tip) to represent handles. Attach the doors to the edge of the dresser by rolling small lengths of paste to fit the doors. Stick these to the dresser, then attach the doors, supporting them with foam sponge until dry.

Christmas Tree

Use the three length guides on page 97 to cut pieces of 24-gauge wire. Make a short right angle bend in each piece and place on runout film. Using a no. 1 piping tube (tip) and green royal icing, pipe small leaves down one side of the wire, pulling away as you release the pressure to give the shape. Pipe along the opposite side of the wire, in between the spaces. Repeat along the top of the wire and leave to dry. Then turn the wire over and repeat on the reverse side to give four lines of piped needles. Repeat for the other pieces of the wire to make the branches for the tree. Allow the branches to dry for 12 hours.

Shape a cylinder of modelling paste for the trunk. Cut a groove in the back and insert a piece of 24-gauge green wire. Bring the paste up around the wire, then turn the paste over so that the join is at the back. Mark a few lines on the trunk, then use angled tweezers to hook the end of each branch into the

trunk, starting from the base. Decrease the size of the branches as you work towards the tree top. Place the tree in position on the cake and adjust the angles of the branches. Pipe around points where the branches enter the tree trunk with green royal icing. Pipe on any needles which have fallen off during this process, then allow the tree to dry.

Roll out modelling paste for the tub and cut out, then allow to dry. Shape a small piece of brown paste to represent soil and shape it around the base of the trunk. Cover the tub with green paste and shape the front so that it is rounded. Paint on the design when dry. Secure the tree into the tub with sugar glue. then allow to dry.

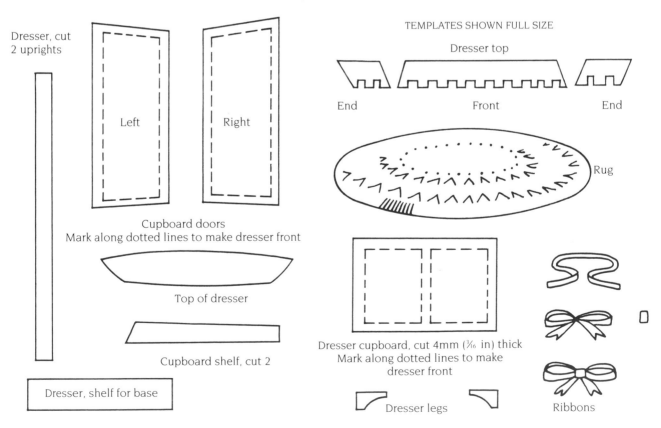

TEMPLATES SHOWN FULL SIZE

Dresser, cut 2 uprights

Left

Right

Cupboard doors
Mark along dotted lines to make dresser front

Top of dresser

Cupboard shelf, cut 2

Dresser, shelf for base

Dresser top

End   Front   End

Rug

Dresser cupboard, cut 4mm (³⁄₁₆ in) thick
Mark along dotted lines to make
dresser front

Dresser legs   Ribbons

Mother Rabbit

Place the templates for the rabbit, see page 139, in a clear plastic file. Model the head and body over the templates. The arms are made as shown for the marzipan characters, see page 36, but smaller. Paint the details on the head when the paste is dry.

Roll out a piece of flower paste thinly, then cut a small rectangle to waist height on the rabbit. Gather this to form the skirt. Roll out the paste and cut the top of the dress. Secure to the rabbit. Cover the arms with thinly rolled paste, then stick them to the body and support with pieces of foam sponge until dry. Roll white flower paste and cut out the apron. Flute the edges with a ball tool and attach to the waist with sugar glue. Repeat for the top of the apron. Add a waist band and a bow at the back.

Secure the head to the body. Use powder food colouring to add a little colour to the dress.

▲ *The stages used to build up the mother rabbit.*

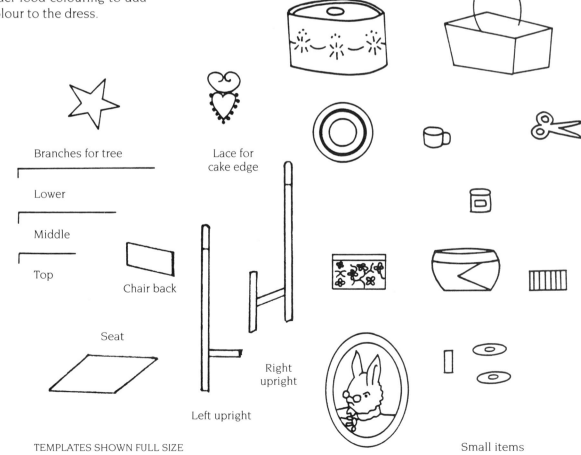

Branches for tree

Lower

Middle

Top

Chair back

Seat

Lace for
cake edge

Left upright

Right
upright

Small items

TEMPLATES SHOWN FULL SIZE

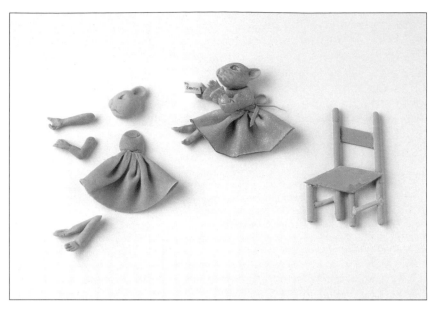

Mouse and Chair

Model the mouse (see templates on page 139) as for the rabbit but the dress forms the body when the rectangle of paste is gathered together. The legs are stuck on the inside of the skirt with sugar glue. Brush the skirt with sparkle petal dust when dry.

Roll pieces of paste for the chair, then shape on the edge of the dresden modelling tool. Cut to length and allow to dry. Cut the back and seat of the chair using the template on page 97. Secure all of the pieces together with soft green royal icing, then allow to dry for 12 hours.

Small Items

Cups, Plates and Boxes

Hollow a small piece of modelling paste over the end of a paintbrush to make a cup. Trim the edge of the cup while the paste is still on the paintbrush. Cut a small strip of paste for the handle, fold both ends over then stick it to the side of the cup.

Roll the paste thinly for the plates and cut out circles with the wide end of a piping tube (tip).

Shape the boxes from small rectangles of modelling paste, marking on the indents with a scalpel blade.

Paint on the details when dry, holding the pieces with tweezers as you paint.

Picture

Cut out the oval shape from thinly rolled modelling paste, then leave to dry. Trace the picture onto the

oval and paint it with food colouring. Roll a strip of paste to go around the outside and stick it to the edge of the oval. Mark on a groove with a scalpel around the edge. Attach to the wall when dry, then pipe a line to resemble the picture wire.

Basket

Roll out the modelling paste thinly and cut it out using the template. Cut thin strips of paste and stick them to the side of the basket. Using a no. 00 piping tube (tip), pipe basket weave over the cut strips of paste. Pipe around the top and edge of the basket. Cut a handle and attach it to the top of the basket. When dry dust with powder food colouring.

Cotton Reel and Scissors

The cotton reel is made from two small ovals of paste joined by a small cylinder.

For scissors, roll out the paste and cut two holes for the handles using the tip of a no. 2 piping tube (tip). Cut the shape of the handles around the two holes and cut the blades using a scalpel. When dry, paint both sides with silver powder food colouring mixed with clear alcohol.

Scroll, Mat and Bows

Cut a small rectangle of rolled-out paste for the scroll, then fold opposite ends around cocktail sticks (toothpicks) to dry. Paint on the poem and holly.

Cut out the mat and dry flat. Paint on the design using food colouring. The bows are thin strips of flower paste which have the ends folded over to the centre then folded back again for the tails.

Top View of the Cake

Mix a small amount of flower paste to a soft consistency with a little sugar glue. Secure the small items on the shelves of the dresser. Stick the mat to the floorboards, then add the Christmas tree and secure it with the glue. The bows and the star are stuck to the branches with soft green royal icing.

Position the rabbit in front of the dresser, then support it from behind with a small piece of paste as you secure the feet to the floor. Stick the small mouse to the chair, then position on the cake and secure the legs of the chair with the paste mixture. Allow all the pieces to set.

Add the finishing touches: secure the scissors to the right

hand of the rabbit and allow to dry. Add the basket and secure small pieces of ribbon and small pieces of paste to resemble fir cones. Cut a thin strip of red flower paste, then wrap one end around the cotton reel. Secure the cotton reel to the cake, then drape the other end of the red paste over

---

MODELLING MEMO

The modelled pieces which form the Christmas scene are shaped into the cut out cake. If you separate your picture into different areas of background, middle ground and foreground, then setting them at different levels into the cake, you can create depth which adds another dimension to the finished scene.

---

the blades of the scissors and into the left hand of the rabbit. Add the scroll.

Pipe a garland of green royal icing around the edge of the scene, using the same technique as for the tree branches. Repeat on the side of the cake. Add small red bows.

Lace

Trace the lace template, see page 97, several times and secure under runout film. Use a no. 0 piping tube (tip) and white royal icing to pipe 75 pieces of lace. Leave to dry, then secure around the edge of the cake. Trim the bottom of the cake and board edge with red ribbon.

Victoriana

Marzipan flowers were a popular feature of Victorian sugar work, when they were the focal point on highly decorated plaques with elaborate crimper-work edges. The posy of flowers and traditional pattern on this cushion cake indicate a little of the history of sugar modelling.

INGREDIENTS

20cm (8 in) square cake
875g (1¾ lb) marzipan (almond paste)
Apricot Glaze, see page 14
1.25kg (2½ lb) sugarpaste
selection of food colourings
250g (8 oz) Modelling Marzipan, see page 9

EQUIPMENT

dresden, spade-edged, cone and ball tools
30cm (12 in) square cake board
no. 0, 1 and 2 piping tubes (tips)
paintbrush
ribbon to trim board edge

Trim the corners of cake so that they slope in the shape of a cushion. Brush with apricot glaze and cover with marzipan, see page 14. Coat with sugarpaste, see page 14, and mark the indents in the soft paste with a dresden tool, see diagram on page 139. Cover the board with yellow sugarpaste and dry before placing the cake on it.

Make the flowers and leave them to dry in an airtight container for 12 hours before arranging them on the cake. To complete the cake, scribe a line around the side, 3cm (1¼ in) from the base of the board. Measure the width of the cake and cut a piece of paper to length, then divide it into five equal sections and mark these points on the cake. Using a no. 0 piping tube (tip) and yellow royal icing, pipe two rows of dropped lines between the marked points. Pipe a third row using lilac icing, allowing the icing to fall between each scallop to create the tear drop shape. Neaten the joins between scallops with a

damp paintbrush. Pipe the scallops around the edge of the board with pale lemon royal icing, using a no. 1 piping tube (tip). Trim the board edge with ribbon to contrast with the colours used on the cake.

▲ *Daisy*

Daisy

Take a pea-sized piece of marzipan and flatten it into a circle between two pieces of polythene, thinning the outer edge with your thumb. Use the spade edge of the tool to divide the circle into three. Mark two more sections in each of the three wedges. Then make a small 'V' cut at the edge of the circle on each mark. Pick the daisy shape up on the polythene and carefully shape each petal between your thumb and index finger. Place the daisy on the edge of a rolling board and roll the cone tool from side to side over each petal. Cup the centre with a ball tool. Mould a small cone of white marzipan, then secure the daisy on this using the ball tool. Roll a small ball of yellow-gold marzipan and push it gently into the flower centre. Use a no. 2 piping tube (tip) to mark the centre of the flower to resemble stamens. Adjust the size of the cone at the back of the flower before arranging it in the spray.

▼ *Pansy, opposite*

Pansy

Make a cone of marzipan, then make a smaller cone to fit inside it. Pinch the edges of the marzipan together as you shape the cone, which should be quite flat. Make five cuts into the marzipan with the spade edge of the tool, to give one large and four smaller petals. Pinch the edges of the petals to round them. Place a piece of polythene over one petal and apply even pressure to thin the edge.

Repeat on the remaining petals.

Make a small crescent shape of contrasting marzipan, then place it in the centre of the largest petal. Smooth down with the edge of the dresden tool, making five or six small lines radiating from the centre. Make a small stamen from green marzipan and insert it into the centre. Vary the colours of the pansies for variety in an arrangement.

For a leaf, make a small cone of marzipan and thin the edge of the

paste between polythene. Push in the edges of the paste with a dresden tool to shape the leaf. Mark the veins, then shape the leaf and allow to set.

Dahlia

Colour the marzipan three shades of yellow-gold. Roll the lightest colour to 1mm (1/16 in) thick and cut out a 5cm (2 in) circle. Place the circle on a piece of polythene. Roll

▲ *Dahlia*

the lightest colour into a small cylinder shape and cut off small pieces. Place a piece of marzipan between polythene and thin it gently with your thumb into a circle measuring about 1.5cm (¾ in) in diameter. Roll the circle into a cone and place this on the 5cm (2 in) circle of marzipan, overlapping the edge by 2mm (scant ⅛ in). Continue making cones to cover the circle in a neat ring. Use the next shade of marzipan to make another row of cones. Continue building up rows of cones until you fill the entire circle, graduating the colour so that the centre of the flower is darker than the outside. Place in an airtight container to set for 12 hours.

Make a 2.5cm (1 in) cone of white marzipan and flatten the top. Place this under the dahlia to give it height when arranged with the other flowers.

Rose

Colour 30g (1 oz) marzipan deep gold, then cut the paste in half and mix one portion with an equal amount of white marzipan. Repeat once more to give three tints of yellow. Use the darkest for the centre of the rose and the first three petals. The next shade for the next three petals and the lightest for another five petals.

The rose can be made larger by using more marzipan. If the rose

petals fall back after they are modelled, the marzipan has probably been thinned too much down the whole petal shape instead of just at the edge. It is important to graduate the thickness of the petal by stroking the marzipan from the base of the petal to the edge where more pressure should be applied.

Stages for Making a Rose

Shape a cone from the darkest shade of marzipan. For the first three petals, roll the darkest colour into a small cylinder and cut off three pieces for petals. Thin the marzipan between two pieces of polythene by stroking it gently. Start at the point which will be the base of the petal, then apply more pressure as you stroke the edge of the paste which will be the top edge of the petal.

Wrap the first petal around the cone, taking care not to place it too low on the cone, otherwise you will expose the centre of the cone.

▼ *Making a rose.*

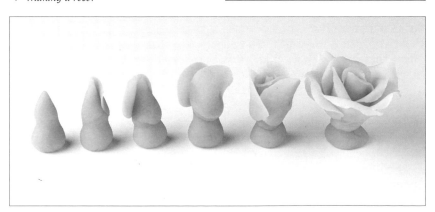

Position the next two petals opposite each other around the cone. Make sure that the edges of the petals interlock around the cone and gently fold back their edges to give the flower movement. Repeat for the next three petals using the lightest shade of marzipan. Leave the rose at this stage for a bud – squeeze the base and cut off the excess marzipan.

To complete a large rose, continue with the lightest shade of marzipan and add another five petals. When you position the first petal, leave its outside edge free, so that you can interlock the outside edge of the fifth petal underneath it. Carefully squeeze the rose around the base to remove the excess marzipan and trim it off with a knife. Allow the rose to set in an airtight container overnight, then, if you wish, airbrush the edges for a more intense colour.

MODELLING MEMO

Most people who have made flowers from flower paste try to use the same techniques when modelling with marzipan but the paste is far softer and the texture and finish is different, so the approach is not the same. When well modelled, marzipan flowers have a superb lustre and the edges of the petals can be translucent. Before you start, it is important to ensure that all the colours required are mixed and that all equipment is clean.

I Wish

When modelling children, the adult form is simplified and animated features applied to create the child-like charm and character which is so appealing.

INGREDIENTS

23cm (9 in) round cake
Apricot Glaze, see page 14
1kg (2 lb) marzipan (almond paste)
1.25kg (2½ lb) sugarpaste
selection of food colourings
clear alcohol (vodka or gin)
60g (2 oz) Flower Paste, see page 8
155g (5 oz) Modelling Paste, see
    page 8
small amount of Rock Sugar, see
    page 8
spaghetti

EQUIPMENT

30cm (12 in) round cake board
small and medium daisy cutters
no. 1 piping tube (tip)
ribbon for board edge
dog bone and dresden modelling tools
cocktail sticks (toothpicks)
Garrett frill cutter

Brush the cake with apricot glaze and cover with marzipan. Leave to dry. Cover the cake board with white sugarpaste; leave to dry. Colour the remaining sugarpaste peach. Brush the cake with alcohol and cover with peach sugarpaste and leave to dry. Position the cake on the board.

Using the daisy cutters, stamp out 16 open daisies in thinly rolled flower paste. Make a further five half daisies and six small daisies. Gently lift and curve the petals of the daisies, so that they look realistic. Pipe soft royal icing in their centres and sprinkle with semolina coloured with a little yellow powder food colouring.

Model the wall for the base of the cake from pieces of modelling paste, following the notes on stones, see page 39. Flatten the stones and arrange them irregularly around the cake, attaching them with sugar glue. Paint the stems for the daisies and leaves, and plants following the template on page 106 as a guide. Attach the daisies and paint the leaves freehand, using the template on page 106 as a guide. Pipe the curved lines between the daisies using green royal icing and a no. 1 piping tube (tip).

Brush soft royal icing around the base of the cake. Colour some rock sugar with brown powder food colouring and crush it, then sprinkle it around the base of the cake, on the royal icing. Secure the figure and the rag doll to the cake and trim the board edge with ribbon.

Figure

Use the diagram on page 104 as a guide to proportions for modelling the figure.

▼ *Making the figure and doll.*

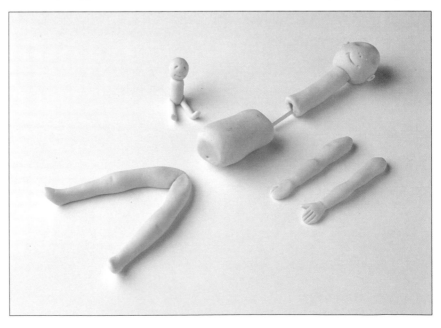

Head

Roll a ball of flesh-coloured modelling paste for the head. Indent the eye shape using a dog bone tool. Mark the curve of the mouth with the edge of a piping tube (tip), then make two small indents at the corners of the mouth for dimples. Mark two dots for the nose with the veining end of a dresden tool.

Roll a cylinder of modelling paste for the neck. Insert a piece of spaghetti into the cylinder, then push it into the head. Brush sugar glue around the neck so that it will stick in place.

Roll two small pieces of paste for ears, position them on the head and indent the centre of each with a dresden tool. Cover a spare piece of sugarpaste with cling film (plastic wrap). Puncture a small hole in the cling film. Push the end of the spaghetti protruding from the head into the spare sugarpaste and leave to dry.

Paint on the eyes, starting with

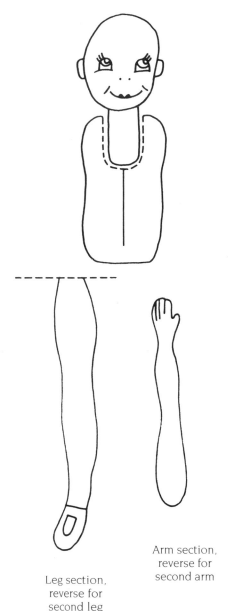

Leg section,
reverse for
second leg

Arm section,
reverse for
second arm

leg and the knee joints. Bend the ends of the paste around and shape feet, making them wider and shorter than those for an adult. Fold the legs in half and position them on the body.

Assembling the Figure

The figure is placed on the edge of the cake to dry in the correct position. Shape an arm by rolling a cylinder of paste, then round the hand end and cut a 'V' for the thumb and three cuts for fingers.

Leave the fingers together but adjust the shape of the thumb by rolling the end between your thumb and index finger. Model a small rim around the wrist to make the arm appear chubby by rolling the paste on the edge of a cutting board. Repeat for the other arm. Stick both arms on the body with water so that they dry in the required position. Leave for 24 hours, then remove the arms and dress them separately as shown. Paint the socks with cut-out section for the shoe.

▼ *Making curls for hair.*

an oval shape in white, then adding small brown circles for the pupils. Paint a small black semi-circle over each pupil for an iris. Paint a small semi-circle for the top lip.

Body

Model the body and hollow the centre. Insert the neck and head into the body and mould the paste around the neck to secure it in place.

Roll a cylinder of paste for the legs as they are shaped in one piece. Roll the paste on the edge of one finger to curve the top of the

Curls

Colour some modelling paste light brown and roll it out thinly. Roll out and cut rectangles about 12 x 3mm (⅜ x ¼ in). Mark lines on the paste using the edge of a palette knife. Lift the paste, then roll the ends in opposite directions to form the curls. Roll sufficient curls of various sizes to cover the head – about 20 – 25 pieces. Secure the curls with light brown royal icing, facing in different directions on the head. A single curl can be made by twisting a thin strip of paste around a cocktail stick (toothpick). Moisten one end of the paste, then place it on the head. Gently remove the cocktail stick in an upwards direction as the curl falls free.

Rag Doll

A small rag doll is modelled from flesh-coloured modelling paste, with the head attached directly on the body and the legs rolled separately, then secured to the body.

Dressing the Figure and Rag Doll

Roll out pale blue flower paste and cut out the dress using the templates on page 67 as a guide and trimming the paste to fit. Secure the back and front of the dress. Cut out a skirt using a Garrett frill cutter. Frill the edges of the skirt by rolling a cocktail stick (toothpick) on the edge of the paste. Cut the paste in as far as the centre. Gather the paste around the waist of the figure and secure it in place.

Cut a small section of white paste for the smocking and mark with a veining end of the dresden tool. Pinch the marked lines together with small tweezers to form the shape of the smocking and leave to dry. Paint on the lines to represent stitches when dry.

Add a waistband and small bow at the back of the dress, cut from strips of rolled-out flower paste.

Roll out flower paste thinly and cut a small rectangle for the rag doll's dress, trimming it to fit. Cut down the back of the paste and shape it around the body. Make two small arms and insert them under the edges of the dress paste which represent sleeves.

Finishing the Model and Cake

Brush the figure's cheeks with a little pink powder food colouring to give them a blush. Paint the face on the rag doll. Cut thin strips of

hair for the rag doll or use a fine mesh on a clay gun to extrude hair.

Position the figure and the rag doll on the cake with sugar glue. Glaze the ladybirds with confectioners' glaze when they are in position.

▲ *The figure and rag doll with the stages for their clothes.*

Top design

Ladybird

Side design

Gazebo

An elegant gazebo sheltering doves of peace on a central column makes an excellent centrepiece for a formal cake and here it is displayed on a hexagonal cake, decorated completely in white.

INGREDIENTS

185g (6 oz) Pastillage 1, see page 8
20cm (8 in) hexagonal cake
Apricot Glaze, see page 14
875kg (1¾ lb) marzipan (almond paste)
1.25kg (2½ lb) Royal Icing, see page 9

EQUIPMENT

6.5cm (2½ in) round cutter
large rose petal cutter
felt-tip pen
dresden tool
fine emery board
no. 1 piping tube (tip)
paintbrush
30cm (12 in) hexagonal board
pink ribbon for board edge

This form of modelling is similar to any other precise construction work, where all the sections must be cut accurately in order to fit together when dry. It is difficult to trim excess off dried pastillage but the pieces for the gazebo are cut thinly, so it is possible to cut off small pieces if the surface of the dried paste is scored lightly with a sharp scalpel blade. Alternatively, any excess can be sanded off using a fine emery board.

Gazebo

Trace all the templates, see pages 108 and 111, and cut them out in thin card. Roll out the pastillage to 1mm (¹⁄₁₆ in) thick for all sections. A 3cm (1¼ in) round cutter is useful for cutting the curves smoothly and a rose petal cutter is used for the teardrop sections on the top of the gazebo. When all the sections are cut, leave to dry for 24 hours.

Columns

Using the template on page 111 as a guide, roll a cylinder of paste to the required size. Make sure that the length of pastillage rolls freely on the surface, then hold the blade of a knife at a 45° angle across the pastillage and roll the blade towards you to mark a spiralling ring around the pastillage. Roll the paste back and forth to cut evenly through the cylinder without squashing the paste. Leave to dry flat on foam sponge.

▲ *Cutting the top sections.*

Plinth

Roll a rectangle of pastillage long enough to wrap around the barrel of a felt-tip pen. Mark vertical lines on the pastillage, about 1mm (¹⁄₁₆ in) apart using a veining tool and holding a ruler as a guide for keeping the marks straight. Cut the paste to 5cm (2 in) long, wrap it around the pen and lay it on its side to dry. Cut four hexagonal

▼ *Marking the spiral on a column. The paste is also cut ready for making the plinth.*

MODELLING MEMO

When cutting pastillage for construction modelling or flat modelling, use a large, clean sharp kitchen knife with a blade measuring about 18 - 20 cm (7 - 8 in) long. Cut on the reverse of your rolling board, to avoid damaging the surface of the board, and use a guillotine action to cut. Do not drag the knife blade.

Keep all trimmings together in a polythene bag and re-roll them together. This prevents the pastillage from becoming too dry and turning an off-white.

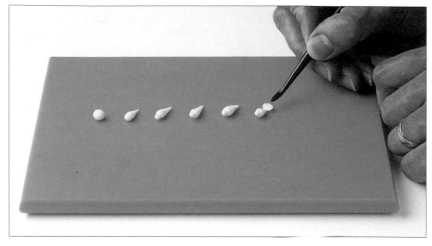

▲ *Making the doves.*

pieces for the top and base of the plinth and leave to dry. Assemble the plinth when dry, securing the pieces with royal icing.

Doves

Roll a pea-size piece of pastillage into an elongated cone shape. Roll the edge of the dresden tool on the widest end to form the head. Then adjust it so that it sits back on the body. Mark the tail by rolling the pastillage on the edge of the dresden tool. Fold the tail point under and press it with the dresden tool so that it fans out. Lift the tail a little and leave it to dry. Position the doves on the plinth and secure them with a little royal icing. Make a piece of laurel as for the leaves on page 46, and attach it to the beak of one dove.

ENLARGE ALL TEMPLATES TO 118% ON A PHOTOCOPIER

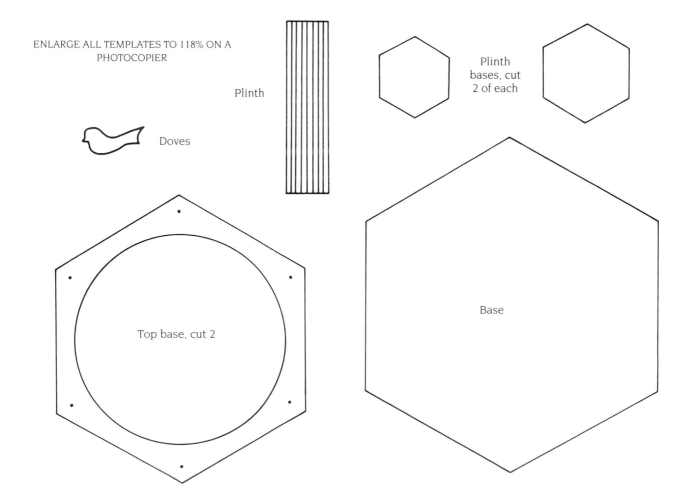

Plinth

Plinth bases, cut 2 of each

Doves

Top base, cut 2

Base

Assembling the Gazebo

Check that all the edges are smooth by gently sanding them with a fine emery board. Use soft white royal icing and a no. 1 piping tube (tip) to join the sections together. Brush any surplus icing from the joins with a damp paintbrush. Support the pieces with foam sponge as they are assembled. The gazebo should be assembled in the following sequence.

1 Join all the side panels to the base hexagon.

2 Assemble the triangular pieces for the top, ensuring the edges of the triangles are not outside the top hexagon.

3 Fit and secure all the sections around the top hexagon, placing the top hexagon on a small circle of foam sponge so that the side pieces can be added. Leave to dry for 12 hours.

4 Turn the top piece upside down and support it in a glass or suitable container. Measure the columns – it is important that they are all exactly the same length otherwise the gazebo will not stand correctly. Smooth down any rough edges. Pipe royal icing into the corners of the top hexagon, then place the columns in their upright position. Check that the columns are straight before leaving to dry for 24 hours.

5 Secure the base circle to the base hexagon.

6 Attach the doves to the plinth. Place the plinth on the centre of the base.

MODELLING MEMO

To transfer cut-out pieces to a drying board, slide a sheet of paper under them. Turn the pieces over during drying to prevent them from buckling. Always ensure that the pieces are thoroughly dry before assembling them, otherwise disaster is inevitable.

▲ *Supporting the gazebo on a glass while attaching the columns.*

7 Pipe royal icing on the bottom of each column, then carefully secure it to the base of the gazebo. Roll a small piece of pastillage into a thin cone to make the spire, leave to dry, then position on the top of the gazebo. Leave to dry for 12 hours before moving. To lift the model, place your fingers around opposite columns.

The Cake

Brush the cake with apricot glaze, cover with marzipan for royal icing, see page 14, and leave to dry. Apply several coats of royal icing, see page 15 and leave to dry. Coat the board with royal icing.

Cut a strip of paper to fit the side of the cake. Fold it into six and draw the two scallops and half a point on each section. Cut out, then open and use this template to mark the cake side. A similar template should be made to mark the design on the top of the cake. Cut a template for the board and mark the scallops in the same way.

The area inside the lines marked from the templates is covered with piping worked in a continuous filigree line. Use a no. 1 piping tube (tip) and curve the piping without breaking it until the area is filled. This is piped on the board as well as on the cake side and top.

Neaten the edge of the pattern by piping a single line of icing. Pipe two more lines, one on each side. Pipe two lines on top to build up the height and add a final line to complete the design. A built-up line of icing is also piped around the top edge of the cake. The bottom edge is finished with beading.

The lace for the top edge is piped on runout film using a no. 1 piping tube (tip). Trace the template below, and check that it fits the cake sides once they are coated with royal icing. Secure the template under the film. Pipe the lace and leave to dry. Position on the cake carefully, attaching it with a line of soft royal icing. Finish by decorating the board with ribbon.

> **MODELLING MEMO**
>
> A *pizza wheel is ideal for cutting straight lines in pastillage, giving a clean cut and neat edge*

ENLARGE ALL TEMPLATES TO 118% ON A PHOTOCOPIER

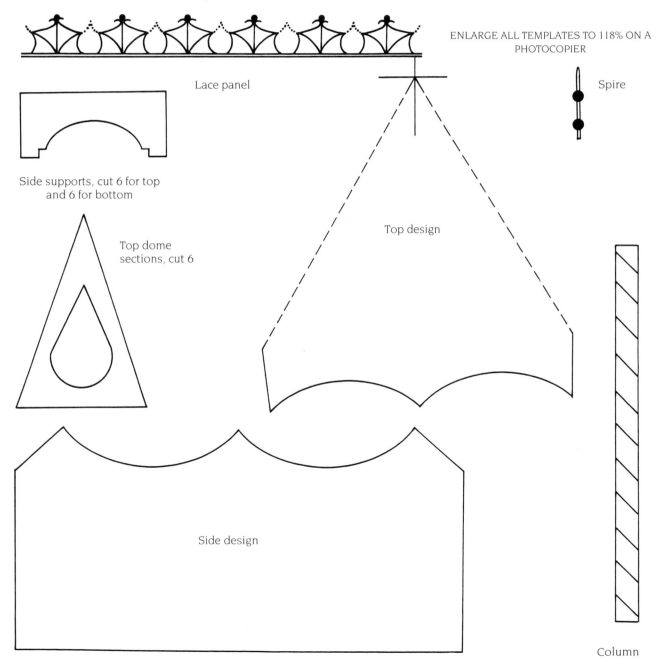

Lace panel

Side supports, cut 6 for top and 6 for bottom

Top dome sections, cut 6

Top design

Spire

Side design

Column

Water Maiden

The flower container and side moulding add a classical air to this dramatic wedding cake. The water theme is carried through by the flowing royal icing design leading from the water jars to the stylized water lilies on the lower tier, and the design is complemented by the arrangement of abstract flower forms.

INGREDIENTS

15cm (6 in) round cake
25cm (10 in) round cake
Apricot Glaze, see page 14
2.25kg (4½ lb) marzipan (almond paste)
2kg (4 lb) sugarpaste
selection of food colourings
clear alcohol (vodka or gin)
250g (8 oz) Pastillage 1 or 2, see page 8
small amount of Royal Icing, see page 9
125g (4 oz) Modelling Paste, page 8
185g (6 oz) Flower Paste, see page 8
white vegetable fat (shortening)
2 teaspoons gelatine
3½ teaspoons water

EQUIPMENT

23cm (9 in) cake board
36cm (14 in) round cake board
length of 1 cm (½ in) wooden dowel
umbrella mould
foam sponge
small pieces of polystyrene
no. 1 piping tube (tip)
empty film container
ornamental wooden moulding
modelling clay
fine emery board
about 20 pieces white 30-gauge wire
4 pieces green 24-gauge wire
runout film
green and white florists' tape
1.2m (1¼ yd) of 3mm (⅛ in) wide peach ribbon
1.6m (1¾ yd) each of green and cream 3mm (⅛ in) wide ribbon
coloured lustre colours
3m (3¼ yd) of 1cm (½ in) picot edge cream ribbon for board edge
acrylic cake stand

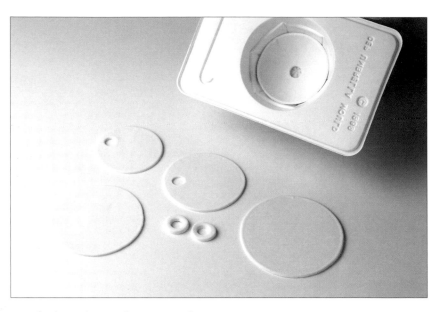

Brush the cakes with apricot glaze and cover with marzipan, see page 14. Colour the sugarpaste cream. Brush the cake with alcohol and cover with the sugarpaste. Cover the boards with sugarpaste. Place the cakes on the boards when the sugarpaste has dried.

Flower Holder

The flower holder may be used on a variety of cakes, to display sugar,

▲ *Using an umbrella mould to make the flower holder.*

silk or dried flowers. Colour the pastillage light cream, then roll it out to the thickness shown by the diagram on page 117. Cut out the four circles for the base, cutting the small circle in the two upper circles of paste for the dowel to be inserted when dry.

▼ *The column is made by wrapping pastillage around wooden dowel.*

Check that the dowel fits in the small circle before leaving the pastillage to dry. Cut the two base supports. Turn the bases partway through drying.

Roll out the pastillage for the flower holder. Cut out the circle for the dish and cut the small circle from the centre. Place the paste in the umbrella mould. Ease the pastillage into the mould without any folds, then check that the dowel fits into the central hole. Leave to dry for 24 hours.

Column

Cut a 17cm (6½ in) length of wooden dowel. Roll out the pastillage to 2.5mm (scant ¼ in) thick, then cut a 14.2cm (5⅝ in) long rectangle wide enough to fit around the dowel. Fold the paste around the dowel, securing it with sugar glue. Cut the pastillage so that it butts together exactly. Dry on a piece of foam sponge for 12 hours, supporting the ends of the dowel between two pieces of polystyrene held in place at each end with two pins to stop it from rolling. Pipe the filigree pattern using cream royal icing and a no. 1 piping tube (tip).

▼ *Making the pots and seat.*

Pots and Seat for Figure

Re-roll the pastillage and cut a narrow strip. Wrap the strip of pastillage around the empty film container. Butt the edges together, sticking them with sugar glue. Cut a small circle, stick it to the base then allow to dry.

Pots

Shape a small pot from a ball of soft pastillage, hollowing out the centre with your fingers, rather like making a small thumb pot in clay. When the hollow pot is the right height, mould the paste inwards for the top edge. Trim the top edge of the pot with scissors. Leave to dry. Roll a small cylinder of pastillage and shape this around the top edge of the pot to make the rim. Make a second pot in the same way.

When the pots and seat are dry, pipe filigree over them as for the column.

Figure

Use modelling paste to make the figure. Follow the instructions on page 46 for making a mould for the head, then make the top of the body. When the top is dry, model the legs as shown on page 43. The

▲ *The figure is dried in a sitting position on the container used to make the seat.*

legs will be covered, so it is only necessary to form the basic shape. Attach the legs to the body, sitting the figure on the seat to dry in the correct position and leave for 12 hours.

Cut a white skirt section, as shown on page 67, then add the top of the dress. Attach six small pieces at the back of the dress so that they fold under the sitting figure. It is best to shape the arms after dressing the figure as they can then be fixed temporarily to the figure to dry in the correct pose. See page 44 for shaping the arms and hands.

Add the longer sections of hair before the arms. Roll the paste into a small cylinder, make small cuts into this with a scalpel, then twist the paste and secure it to the head. Dust with colour.

Secure the arms to the figure, then cut thin strips of flower paste for the flowers in her hands. These are finished as shown on page 45. Dust the edges of the dress with powder food colouring. Secure the figure to the seat. The seat is secured to the base of the flower stand when the flower arrangement is complete.

Side Moulding

The decorative pieces on the cake side are modelled using purchased wooden moulding. Rub the wooden moulding with white vegetable fat (shortening), then press it firmly into a piece of modelling clay. Remove the wood and harden the clay in the oven, following the packet instructions. Wash the hardened mould before use, then grease it lightly with white vegetable fat. Colour some pastillage cream and rub the surface with white vegetable fat before pushing it into the mould. Remove excess paste to leave the top level, then remove the pastillage from the mould. The pieces should be attached to the flower dish immediately, so that the paste can be curved; the pieces for the side of the cake should be dried. The sections on the top tier are cut smaller than those on the bottom tier.

Secure the moulded sections around the dish with cream royal icing. Pipe around the edges of each piece to fill any gaps, then pipe filigree over the dish. Secure a small cylinder of pastillage around the top of the flower holder with sugar glue to neaten the rim.

Assembling the Flower Holder

Rub off any rough edges from the bases with fine emery board, then secure them to each other with royal icing, using the template as a guide. Position the two base supports over the dowel column. Pipe royal icing into the hole on the base and insert the dowel. Pipe runny royal icing over the two base supports and around the base of the dowel. Ensure that the dowel is

upright, then pipe filigree over the base supports. Leave to dry for 12 hours.

Stylized Paste Flowers

The flowers are modelled with a wire edge, shaped around a cutter, then covered with paste, see templates on page 140. Carefully bend 30-gauge wire around the outside of the cutter and twist the ends together, ensuring a tight and neat twist where the two pieces join. Make a wire shape for each flower:

Top Decoration

  8 x size 1
  8 x size 2
  8 x size 3
  6 x size 4

Bottom Tier Decoration

  2 x size 1
  5 x size 2
  6 x size 3
  7 x size 4

Roll out the coloured flower paste thinly, then place it over the a shaped wire section. Roll the paste on the wire to secure it in place and cut away excess paste at the same time. If the paste does not have sufficient stretch, dampen the wire with a little water before rolling the paste over it. Allow the shapes to dry, then colour both sides of each with lustre powder food colouring.

Gelatine Flowers

Begin by making the wire shapes as for the paste flowers:

Top Decoration

  1 x size 1
  3 x size 2
  2 x size 3
  3 x size 4

Bottom Tier Decoration

  3 x size 4

Sprinkle the gelatine over the water in a heatproof basin – do not stir the mixture. Leave for 15 minutes, until the gelatine has

▲ *Making paste flowers.*

sponged, then stand the basin over a saucepan of simmering water until the gelatine has dissolved completely, stirring occasionally.

Lay wire shapes onto a piece of runout film, making sure that each wire is lying perfectly flat. Carefully brush the dissolved gelatine into the wire shapes using a medium paintbrush. Leave to set – this will take 5 – 10 minutes. Then peel the wire from the film. Leave the gelatine to set hard, then brush with lustre powder food colouring.

▼ *Making gelatine flowers.*

Assembling the Arrangement

Cover four pieces of 24-gauge wire with green tape, then wrap coloured ribbon around each piece and secure with glue to give the two-colour result. Twist the wires into the curved shapes for the arrangement.

Tape together alternate colours and graduating sizes of the flowers to form the two main curves of the display. Then tape two and three flower shapes together to form smaller sprays.

Take a ball of pastillage about the size of a walnut, then work in a little extra carboxymethyl cellulose until the paste tightens. Secure this paste in the flower holder, so that the dowel fits into the centre of the paste. Fit the flower holder onto the dowel support and secure with softened pastillage and sugar glue. Position the four curves of covered wire into the paste, hooking their ends before you push the sprays of flower shapes into the paste. Hooking the wire prevents it from twisting. Continue adding the flower shapes until the arrangement is complete.

Secure the finished figure to the base of the flower holder and allow to dry for 12 hours before moving.

Completing the Cake

Cut a strip of greaseproof paper (parchment) to fit around each cake side. Fold into six equal sections and draw a scallop across the section. Open out the paper and position it around the cake, then mark the design on the cake. Trace the embroidery on page 140 and mark it on the cake. Pipe the embroidery and scallops using a no. 1 piping tube (tip) and cream royal icing.

Trace the flowing water design for the top of the bottom tier and transfer it to the cake. Pipe it using a no. 1 piping tube (tip) and cream royal icing. Fill the flowing-water shape with filigree piping. The same design is piped on the board of the top tier. Position the pots and pipe small droplets of liquid glucose onto their edges to resemble water.

Insert a plastic flower pick in the paste at the end of the piped design on the bottom cake. Fill the flower pick with pastillage and arrange a group of flowers in it.

MODELLING MEMO

The flower holder makes an attractive wedding cake decoration without the figure, filled with flowers modelled in the colours of your choice.

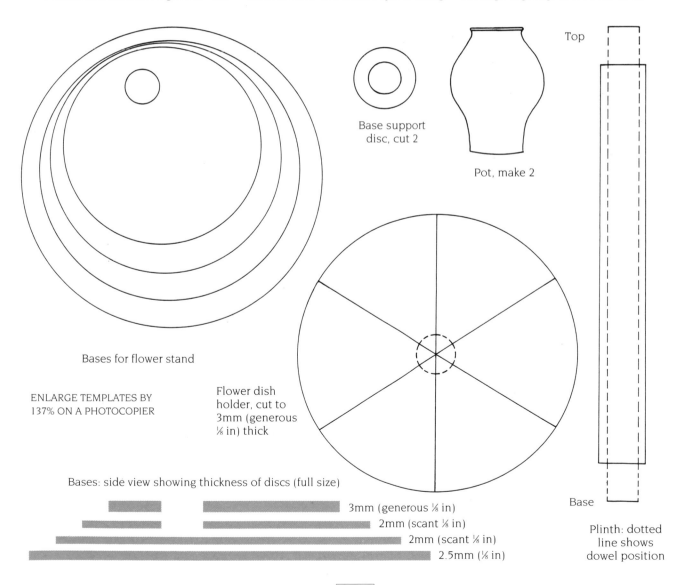

Base support disc, cut 2

Pot, make 2

Top

Bases for flower stand

ENLARGE TEMPLATES BY 137% ON A PHOTOCOPIER

Flower dish holder, cut to 3mm (generous ⅛ in) thick

Bases: side view showing thickness of discs (full size)

3mm (generous ⅛ in)

2mm (scant ⅛ in)

2mm (scant ⅛ in)

2.5mm (⅛ in)

Base

Plinth: dotted line shows dowel position

The Wild West

A fun cake for children, using simple modelling construction and half bas relief techniques. Boiled rock sugar adds an authentic look to the finished cake.

INGREDIENTS

25cm (10 in) long octagon cake
Apricot Glaze, see page 14
1.3kg (2¾ lb) marzipan (almond paste)
clear alcohol (vodka or gin)
1.75kg (3½ lb) sugarpaste
250g (8 oz) Modelling Paste, see page 8
5ml (1 teaspoon) gum tragacanth
small amount of Royal Icing, see page 9
spaghetti
Rock Sugar, see page 8

EQUIPMENT

clear plastic file wallet
dresden tool
small round plunger cutter
no. 2 and 0 piping tube (tip)
cotton thread
foam sponge
airbrush
edible food colouring pens
rice paper
36cm (14 in) long octagon cake board
1.4m (1½ yd) of 1cm (½ in) brown ribbon for board edge

▲ *Making the standing cowboy.*

Brush the cake with apricot glaze. Set aside 250g (8 oz) marzipan for modelling. Use the remainder to cover the cake, see page 14. Brush with alcohol and coat with sugarpaste, see page 14. Cover the board with brown sugarpaste. When dry, position the cake on the board. Use a no. 2 piping tube (tip) and brown royal icing to pipe a border of beading around the base of the cake.

Trace the templates on page 119 and place them in a clear plastic file wallet. Colour the modelling paste flesh tone for the characters, then place it in a polythene bag. Model the characters using the templates in the wallet to check the dimensions and proportions.

Half Bas Relief Standing Cowboy

Shape a ball of modelling paste for the head, then mark the eyes with the dresden tool. Mark the mouth with a small round plunger cutter and make two small indents into the corner of the mouth. Roll a small 'V'-shaped piece of paste for the nose.

Shape a cylinder for the body, then cut and separate a section for the legs. Make a small indent into which to the boots can be fitted. Roll white modelling paste for the shirt and cut a rectangle to fit around the body. Cut out a 'V'-shape for the collar. Place this over the body and fold back the edges of the collar.

Secure the head to the body with sugar glue, then roll a small piece of paste and shape it over the head for the hair. Roll two very small pieces of paste for the ears and secure them to the head, indenting them as you attach them with the dresden tool.

Roll two small cylinders of paste for the arms. Stick one arm to the side of the body. Make a small hollow at the end of the other arm to fit a hand. Make the hand from a small oval-shaped piece of paste, marking on the fingers. Cut a triangle of paste for the gun, then stick it to the hand and secure the hand into the hollow at the end of the arm.

Shape two tear-drop pieces of paste for the boots and stick them to the indents at the end of the trousers. Mould the hat from a small ball of paste, pinching out the edge, then shape it over the head and secure it with sugar glue.

Paint small black dots for the eyes and a little brown diluted food colour onto the chin for stubble. Paint the waistcoat and leave to dry completely.

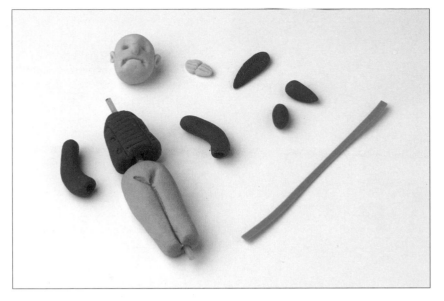

Indian

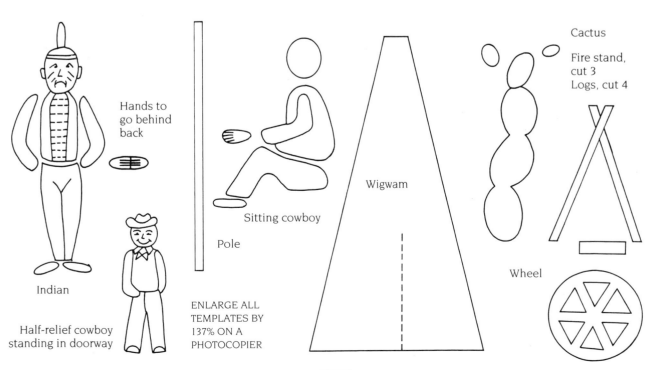

Use the same flesh-tone modelling paste for the Indian. Shape an elongated cone for the legs, making a cut to the back and front. Insert a length of spaghetti down the length of each leg. Shape the top of the body, then mark on the jacket and the button holes with the end of a no. 2 piping tube (tip). Insert a piece of spaghetti into the body, leaving about 1cm (½ in) protruding for the head and 4cm (1¾ in) to insert into the cake.

▲ *Making the Indian*.

Shape the head, then mark the eyes and mouth. Add small pieces of paste for the ears, making a slight indent in each ear as it is attached. Stick the head to the body, then roll very small pieces of paste and stick them into the eye indents.

Shape the boots from two small teardrop shapes of paste, then stick them to the base of the trousers. Cover a spare piece of sugarpaste with cling film (plastic wrap) and puncture the plastic,

then push the Indian into it; leave to dry.

Roll a thin strip of paste and cut a band to go around the Indian's head. Flatten a teardrop-shaped piece of paste and mark lines on it radiating from the middle to resemble a feather. Stick the feather to the back of the Indian's head. Paint the face with food colouring.

Work the gum tragacanth into the marzipan and roll a piece for the stake. Insert a short length of spaghetti in the paste and roll the marzipan so that the spaghetti is hidden, then allow to harden.

Tie the Indian to the pole with cotton thread, then insert the protruding spaghetti into the cake.

Sitting Cowboy

Shape the modelling paste into a cylinder, then fold it in half. Bend the paste to form the knees and the waist. Model a cone shape for the body, sit this on the legs and adjust the angle so that the body is upright.

Mark on the buttons, then secure the body to the legs with sugar glue. Roll an oval of

Hands to
go behind
back

Indian

Half-relief cowboy
standing in doorway

ENLARGE ALL
TEMPLATES BY
137% ON A
PHOTOCOPIER

Pole

Sitting cowboy

Wigwam

Cactus

Fire stand,
cut 3
Logs, cut 4

Wheel

▲ *Making the sitting cowboy.*

modelling paste for the head. Mark the eyes with a dresden tool and the mouth using a small round plunger cutter. Add small pieces of paste for the ears, indenting them as they are secured to the head with a dresden tool.

Roll a small piece of paste for the nose and add tiny pieces of black paste for the eyes. Mould the hair from a squashed oval of paste and secure to the head. Roll a cylinder of paste for the neck tie and thin both ends to a point, then fold them crossing each other as you place the paste around the neck. Secure the neck tie and head together.

Roll two pieces of modelling paste for the arms and hollow out one end of each. Shape two small ovals for hands. Mark on the fingers and stick the hands inside the arms with sugar glue. Bend the arms slightly, then attach them to the body.

Shape the hat from a small ball of paste, pinching it around the outside to form the brim. Hollow the underside of the hat, then fit it on the cowboy's head, bending the brim to shape.

Shape the box from a cube of marzipan and mark lines on it to resemble the wooden sections.

Rocks

Break the rock sugar into pieces when cold and airbrush with colour or use a soft paintbrush to brush with powder food colouring mixed with a little cornflour (cornstarch).

Fire

Roll a length of the modelling paste and cut four short lengths for logs. Roll thinner pieces for the cooking stand. When dry, secure the three pieces together with a small piece of soft paste, then arrange the stand to form a triangle over the fire. Twist pieces of red and yellow paste together for the flames. Stick the logs together with royal icing, then add the flames.

Crumble some of the rock sugar, then colour with black and a little white powder food colouring to form cinders. Moisten the top of the cake and sprinkle the cinders over.

Cactus

Colour some of the modelling paste green and roll it into cylinder shape. Mark into sections for the cactus shape, then press the paste with your fingers to flatten it. Use a dresden tool to shape the joint between each section of cactus. Make small holes over the cactus shape with the veining end of the dresden tool for thorns, which are last. Twist alternate sections of cactus

▼ *Making the rocks and fire.*

slightly in opposite directions.

Make two further pieces of different sizes and five small pieces to add on when you assemble the cactus. Dry the cactus sections on foam sponge for 12 hours. Assemble the clumps of sections together with a mixture of modelling paste and sugar glue. Support the clumps with pieces of foam sponge until set.

Pipe the thorns irregularly into the holes using a no. 0 piping tube (tip) and cream royal icing.

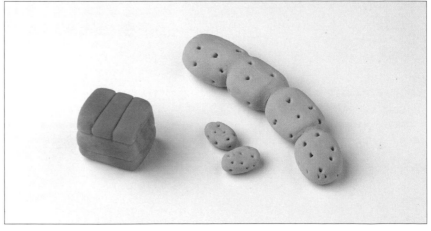

Wheel

Roll the modelling paste to 1 – 2mm ($\frac{1}{16}$ – $\frac{1}{8}$ in) thick and cut out the wheel using the template on page 119. Cut out the centre using the end of a no. 2 piping tube (tip). The spokes may be cut using a small triangle aspic cutter. When dry paint both sides.

Wigwam

Cut out the sections in rice paper, following the template on page 119. Use edible food colouring pens to draw the pattern on the paper, then join the edges of the sections together with water. Avoid putting too much water on as rice paper disintegrates if overdamp.

▲ *Making the wigwam and wheel.*

Saloon and Jail

Cut all the sections for the saloon and jail in marzipan using the templates below and allow to dry on both sides before securing to the side of the cake. Paint the signs.

Paint the landscape around the bottom of the cake and paint the cake surface showing through the door and window. Secure the pieces to the cake with sugar glue. Pipe the bars for the jail using royal icing and a no 0. piping tube (tip).

Secure the half bas relief cowboy in the doorway, then attach the shutters to the edge of the door and around the window. Add the signs.

ENLARGE ALL TEMPLATES BY 137% ON A PHOTOCOPIER

Completing the Cake

Stipple the top of the cake with soft pale brown royal icing using a small piece of natural sponge. Attaching the rocks to the cake with royal icing, then crumble some of the rock sugar and secure it around the base of the cactus.

Position the cowboy, fire and wigwam, securing them with soft royal icing. Trim the board edge with a matching ribbon to complete the cake.

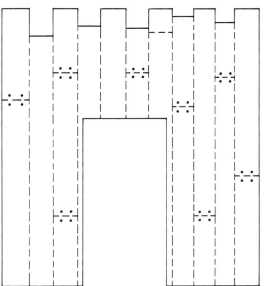

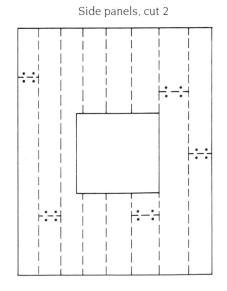

Side panels, cut 2

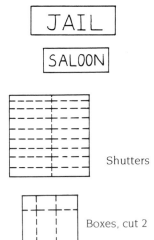

JAIL

SALOON

Shutters

Boxes, cut 2

Snow Queen

A single curve of pastillage represents the background for this model – a free-standing display which could be used for the miniature class of a competition, as the entire model fits within a 15cm (6 in) cube. The model may also be used as the focal point for decorating a cake, with the swirling pattern around the dress repeated around the side of the cake, either by painting or by piping. The dress is cut to represent frost and icicles, and its length means that there is no need to pay attention to modelling legs.

INGREDIENTS

155g (5 oz) Pastillage 1 or 2, see page 8
125g (4 oz) Modelling Paste, see page 8
selection of food colourings
clear alcohol (vodka or gin)
90g (3 oz) Flower Paste, see page 8
small amount of Royal Icing, see page 9

EQUIPMENT

piece of drainpipe
paintbrush
cocktail stick (toothpick)
polystyrene
foam sponge
no. 00 piping tube (tip)
runout film

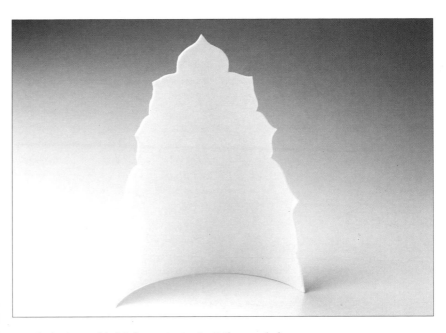

▲ *The background is dried over pipe to give it the curved shape.*

Cut out the background and base templates in thin card, see page 141. Cut the piece of drainpipe in half lengthways. Roll out the pastillage to 1mm (¹⁄₁₆ in) thick and cut out the 14cm (5½ in) base circle. Leave to dry.

Re-roll the paste and carefully cut out the background. Lift the pastillage section on the piece of card, then curve it over the drainpipe to dry for 12 hours. Turn the pastillage regularly during drying, then stand it upright to allow the air to circulate around it. Repeat this process using pale mauve pastillage.

When the base is dry, carefully trace the pattern onto it and paint it with food colouring. When the colouring is dry, attach a disc of thin card underneath the circle with sugar glue.

Figure

Use modelling paste to mould the top of the figure following the instructions on page 42. Allow to dry, then roll a cylinder of paste for the legs. Fold this in half, flatten the folded end and model it onto the top part of the body. Shape the ends of the legs. Insert a cocktail stick (toothpick) into the base of the figure and stand it in a piece of polystyrene to dry for 12 hours.

Paint the eyes and the facial decorations on the figure using food colouring mixed with clear alcohol.

▼ *The basic figure shape.*

▲ *Dressing the figure.*

Dress

Roll out the flower paste to a rectangle large enough to fit around the figure. Bring both ends together at the back, cut off the excess and stick the paste together to form the skirt. Stand the figure upright to ensure that it stands in a well-balanced position.

Cut the dress sections using the templates on page 141. This type of modelling should be quite free, and variations between pieces will make your figure original. Cut the top and back sections and secure them to the model with sugar glue. Mould the arms as shown on page 44 and place them on a piece of foam sponge to dry.

Paint the design on the front of the dress freehand, using the template as a guide. Secure the figure to the base with sugar glue. Then attach the diamonds of thinly rolled flower paste to the dress. The diamonds on the model shown are graduated in colour, from white at the waist to pale mauve at the hemline. To cut the diamonds, cut the paste into strips then cut across at an angle to make diamond shapes. Cut only a few diamonds at a time, as the paste dries quickly and will not stick to the skirt. Secure the diamonds to the skirt with a small amount of sugar glue, overlapping each other.

Cut the sections to go around the neck and waist, then allow to dry before continuing as these small pieces are easily knocked off. Attach the arms with a small amount of soft modelling paste, as shown on page 45. It may be necessary to stand the figure on a piece of polystyrene and support the arms in position until they are dry. Cut the sections from thinly rolled flower paste to go around and under the arms and attach them with sugar glue.

The head-dress has flower paste pieces overlapping down the back of the head. The front piece is cut from flower paste and left to set for a few minutes before placing over the head, otherwise it is likely to fall back.

Paint the small diamond shapes around the neck line and the edges of the sleeve sections. Roll a thin length of flower paste for the wand then dry it on a piece of foam sponge. Cut four small triangles for the top of the wand, then leave them to dry. Paint a line twisting around the wand, then secure the triangles to the end. Secure the wand in the figure's hand with softened paste. Brush the figure with sparkle powder food colouring using a soft brush.

Completing the Model

Secure the background pieces to the base with soft royal icing, removing any surplus with a damp paint brush. Pipe a snow flake using a no. 00 piping tube (tip) and white royal icing on a piece of runout film, and secure it to the other hand of the figure when dry.

▼ *Detail of painting on face.*

River-bank Revelry

The three cakes which are modelled for this theme can be displayed together – the perfect treat for twins' or triplets' birthday parties – or they can be made individually. The cakes are each given a title: Tree-house Mischief, See-saw Games and Caravan Park, so that you can easily select and follow only one set of instructions if you wish.

TREE-HOUSE MISCHIEF

INGREDIENTS

15cm (6 in) round cake
Apricot Glaze, see page 14
1.25kg (2½ lb) marzipan: 375g
   (12 oz) for base covering, plus
   875g (1¾ lb) for effects
2.5ml (½ teaspoon) gum tragacanth
4 pieces of spaghetti
1 hedgehog, see page 31
1 fox, see page 31

EQUIPMENT

dresden tool
1m (1⅛yd) of 1cm (½ in) wide
   green ribbon

SEE-SAW GAMES

INGREDIENTS

part 30cm (12 in) square cake, see
   below, or 20cm (8 in) square
   cake
Apricot Glaze, see page 14
1.6kg (3¼ lb) marzipan: 750g
   (1½ lb) for base covering, plus
   875g (1¾ lb) for effects
a little gum tragacanth
selection of food colourings
1 badger, see page 32
1 frog, see page 33
1 mouse, see page 33

EQUIPMENT

foam sponge
1.4m (1½ yd) of 1cm (½ in) wide
   green ribbon

CARAVAN PARK

INGREDIENTS

part 30cm (12 in) square cake, see
   below
Apricot Glaze, see page 14
3.1kg (6¼ lb) marzipan: 1.25kg
   (2½ lb) for base covering, plus
   1.8kg (3¾ lb) for effects
8.25ml (1⅝ teaspoon) gum
   tragacanth
selection of food colourings
1 rabbit, see page 31
1 weasel, see page 33
1 stoat, see page 34

EQUIPMENT

piece of drain pipe
spade tool
straight frill cutter
3.5cm (2½ in) and 2cm (¾ in) round
   cutters
paintbrush
2m (2⅛ yd) of 1cm (½ in) wide
   green ribbon

Assembling cakes for
Caravan Park

Cutting the whole cake

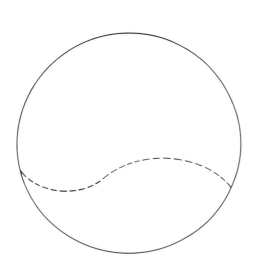

Tree-house Mischief: cutting the cake

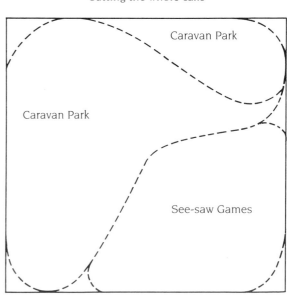

Caravan Park

Caravan Park

See-saw Games

Cutting the Cakes and Cake Boards

Use the templates on page 126 to cut the cakes. If you are making only the See-saw Games cake, then the shape can be cut from a 20cm (8 in) square cake. The cake boards are cut from a piece of plywood and covered with silver cake board foil. Using the templates, right, as a guide, draw around the cake on the plywood and add on a border wide enough for the models.

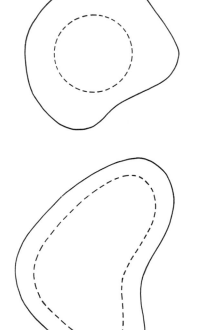

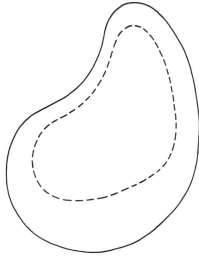

Base board: Tree-House Mischief
25cm (10 in) 25cm (10 in)

Base board: See-saw Games
35cm (13¾ in) 23cm (9 in)

Base board: Caravan Park 50cm
(20 in) 35cm (13¾ in)

Dotted lines show shape of cake on board

Tree-house Mischief

Cut the small curved piece of cake as shown in the template on page 126, then place it on top of the main piece of cake, attaching it with apricot glaze. Brush the cake all over with apricot glaze and cover with marzipan, smoothing the paste over the curves. Cover the board with pale brown marzipan.

Place the cake on the board, then cover it with green marzipan and texture the surface to resemble grass, see page 39. Model stones to complete the decoration on the board, see page 39, and make small plants and pieces of grass to complete the cake, see page 39.

Tree

Knead the gum tragacanth into 250g (8 oz) of the marzipan. Colour the marzipan three different browns and roll the pastes together to give a streaky effect.

Make a cylinder for the trunk from 185g (6 oz) marzipan and model three roots to make a stable base. Carefully insert four lengths of spaghetti into the base of the

▼ *Marking the texture on the tree.*

tree, then push them through into the main branch for added support. Mark the surface of the tree trunk with the widest end of the dresden tool, then use the pointed end to deepen the groves.

Work small pieces of green marzipan into the trunk to give a moss effect. Place the trunk in a polythene bag and leave the marzipan to set for 12 hours. Make sure that you have modelled the trunk into the required shape before leaving it to set, as the marzipan sets firmly with the added gum tragacanth.

Model the branch from a small cylinder of marzipan and divide it further to make smaller branches. Leave the branch to set before fixing it to the main trunk. Insert a small piece of spaghetti into the branch, then join it to the tree trunk with soft marzipan, smoothing the edges to conceal the joins.

Completing the Tree

When the tree has branches and the small pieces of green marzipan added, it is best to fix it to the cake with soft marzipan mixed with a little sugar glue. For the tree stumps, roll different-sized

▼ *The completed tree sections.*

cylinders of marzipan and hollow out their centres slightly. Fill with a lighter marzipan, then texture the top and sides. The trunks have been assembled, one sideways on top of the other, to form a seat for the hedgehog.

Completing the Cake

Make the hedgehog and fox to fit on the cake. Remember to make a small catapult for the hedgehog. When the models are completed and dry, place the fox in his hollow at the front of the cake and sit the hedgehog on the log. Trim the board edge with ribbon.

See-saw Games

Cut the cake using the template on page 126 as a guide. Brush with apricot glaze and cover with marzipan. Place the cake on the board. Cover a small area at the narrow end of the cake with light brown marzipan, from the top edge, down the side and over the board. Cover the rest of the cake and board with green marzipan, smoothing the join with the brown marzipan. Texture the marzipan to represent grass, see page 39, leaving the top of the cake smooth. Make small clumps of grass and tiny flowers as shown, see page 45.

Take a small ball of red marzipan and work a little gum tragacanth into it. Shape the red base for the see-saw by making a rectangular block, then flatten two opposite sides to form the triangular shape.

Roll the marzipan to 4mm (³/₁₆ in) thick, then use the photograph,

right, as a guide to cut out the see-saw plank. Place on a piece of foam sponge to dry. When base and plank are dry, secure as shown on the cake.

Completing the Cake

Model the animals to fit their respective positions on the cake. Place the mouse on one end of the see-saw. The frog is sitting at one end of the cake fishing – remember to make a bright fishing rod for him to hold. The badger is standing by ready to push the see-saw plank for the mouse. When all the animals are modelled and dried, fix them on the cake and trim the board edge with green ribbon.

The badger's hat

(See photograph on page 135). Flatten a small ball of coloured

▲ *Making the see-saw.*

marzipan between two pieces of polythene, thinning the edges slightly more than the centre. Use the veining end of the dresden tool to mark lines radiating from the centre. Repeat the same process for the top of the hat but make this smaller and thicker. Secure both pieces together.

Caravan Park

Use the templates on page 126 to cut the cake. Place the small curved piece towards the back of the cake, attaching it with apricot glaze, then cut a shallow wedge off the front of the cake as shown on the diagram, to make the step in front of which rabbit is standing and on which stoat is sitting.

Brush the cake with apricot glaze and cover with marzipan. Make the boat before covering the board with blue marzipan, then model the water effect around the boat, see page 40.

Cover the cake with green marzipan and model the grass effect, see page 39, leaving small areas of marzipan which should be textured and coloured brown for the edge of the bank. Place the cake on the board and model reeds and water lilies, see pages 39 and 22.

Boat

The boat is made first, so that the water on the board can be modelled around it. Cut out the templates on page 132. Mix three different colours of brown mar-

▲ *Making the boat.*

zipan together to give a wood grain effect. Cut the base of the boat from marzipan rolled out 3mm (⅛ in) thick, then place it on a piece of plastic. Cut a band of marzipan to go around the outside of the

▲ *The assembled boat.*

boat then cover this with cling film (plastic wrap): this will support the shape of the boat.

Roll out the marzipan to about 3mm (⅛ in) thick then mark lines on it, spaced 5mm (¼ in) apart.

Make marks between the lines to resemble staggered planks, then indent the surface with nail holes. Cut a 2.5cm (1 in) strip long enough to go around the outside of the boat. Secure the strip of marzipan around the base edge of the boat; to do this, mix a little of the same marzipan to a paste with sugar glue.

Completing the Boat

Cut the remaining pieces for the boat using the templates below, then leave to set for 12 hours before securing them together with the marzipan paste mixture.

Make the weasel for the boat, see page 33, making the legs small enough for the character to sit in the boat. Make the oars, inserting spaghetti in the handles for extra strength. Model the character's hands so that the oars can be placed in them when they are set, see page 36 for shaping hands to hold objects.

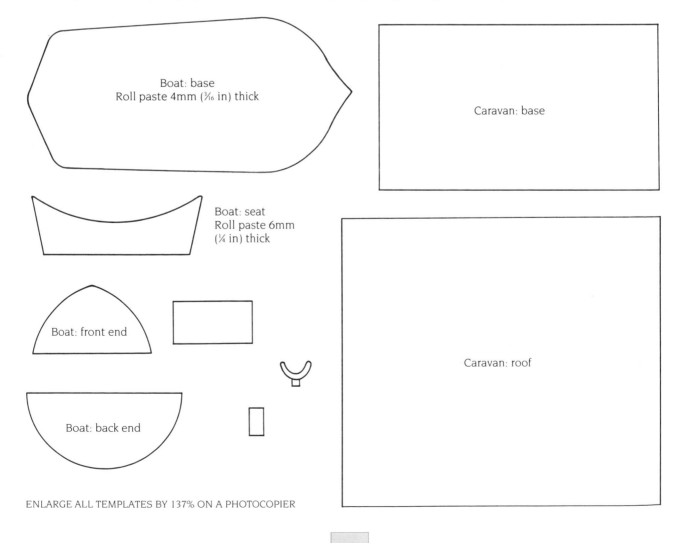

Boat: base
Roll paste 4mm (³⁄₁₆ in) thick

Caravan: base

Boat: seat
Roll paste 6mm
(¼ in) thick

Boat: front end

Boat: back end

Caravan: roof

ENLARGE ALL TEMPLATES BY 137% ON A PHOTOCOPIER

Caravan

The caravan adds height and form to the background scene. Work 5.75ml (1⅛ teaspoons) gum tragacanth into 315g (10 oz) marzipan. This will set the marzipan and make it stronger when assembling the caravan.

Cut the piece of drain pipe in half lengthways. Cut out the sections for the caravan using the templates on pages 132 and below. Use the square end of the spade tool to cut out the windows. Cut the door but leave it in place and dry the pieces on a piece of foam sponge or plywood. Cut a door in different coloured paste to fit and leave to dry. Dry the roof sections on the drain pipe.

Leave all the sections to dry for 1 week, turning them daily to allow

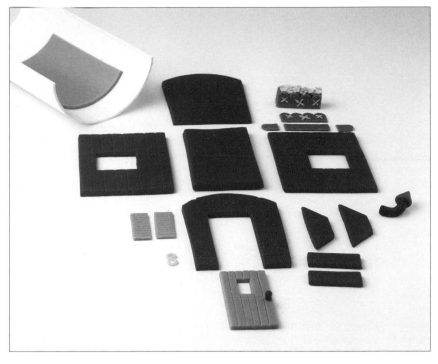

▲ *Making the caravan.*

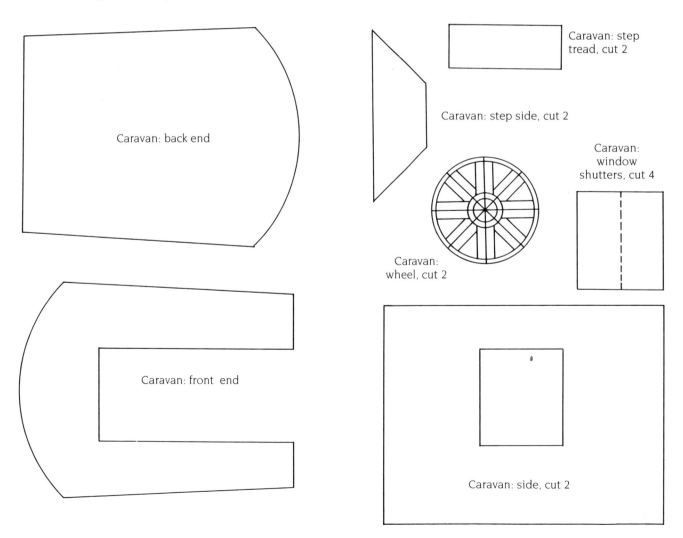

Caravan: back end

Caravan: front end

Caravan: step tread, cut 2

Caravan: step side, cut 2

Caravan: wheel, cut 2

Caravan: window shutters, cut 4

Caravan: side, cut 2

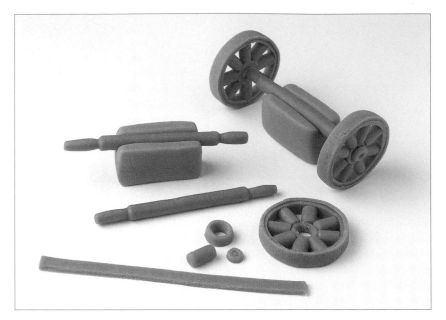

▲ *Wheels for the caravan.*

the air to set both surfaces. You must ensure that all of the sections of the caravan are dry before they are assembled.

To join the sections, mix marzipan with a little sugar glue to make a paste and put it into a piping bag without a piping tube (tip). Snip off just the corner of the bag and pipe the paste along the joint. Remove the excess paste with a small palette knife. Secure the door in place adding small pieces of black marzipan for the hinges.

Use a straight frill cutter to cut out the window boxes. The small flowers on the outside are made by rolling very small pieces of marzipan then securing them to the side. Attach the shutters, then add the window boxes. Roll small lengths of marzipan, then shape them into scrolls and leave to dry. Fix the scrolls on the four corners of the caravan. Shape the chimney and fix it to the side of the caravan, supporting it until it has set.

Wheels

Work 2.5ml (½ teaspoon) gum tragacanth into 125g (4 oz) marzipan. Cut the small rings for the centre of the wheel, cutting the inner one first. The handle of a round plastic cutter fits the size or use the template. Roll small lengths of marzipan for the eight spokes on each wheel and cut them to length by carefully rolling the edge of a palette knife on the marzipan to cut through without squashing it. Allow the spokes to dry, then secure them around the wheel centres with the marzipan and sugar glue paste.

Roll a strip of marzipan long enough to fit around the wheel and wide enough to cover the width of the spokes. Secure the top of each spoke to the strip of paste to make the wheel rim, then leave to dry for 12 hours. Roll a thinner band for the outer wheel rim, using a contrasting colour, then secure it to the outside rim of the wheel. Repeat on the remaining wheels.

Make the axles for the wheels by rolling two cylinders of marzipan. Insert a length of spaghetti in each, then roll until they are thin enough to fit the centre of the wheel. Fix a wheel at each end of each axle.

Axle supports are made to fit underneath the caravan, where they do not show. Model two small blocks of marzipan and indent a groove across each so that the axle will fit into the groove without protruding above the block of paste. Fit the wheels in position on the caravan, then secure the axles on the blocks of marzipan to take the weight of the model. The steps can be placed beneath the door to complete the caravan.

Accessories for Models

The small details make a great difference to a model.

Straw Boater

Cut 3.5cm (2½ in) and 2cm (¾ in) circles of marzipan. Cut a band of marzipan 1cm (½ in) wide to go inside the smaller circle. Place the small circle on top, securing all the edges with sugar glue. Cut a thin strip of thinly rolled marzipan to go around the outside of the hat. The exact size required may vary according to the model.

Picnic Basket

Roll out the marzipan, then cut a rectangular base, two side pieces and two end pieces. Mark lines on the surface of the marzipan. Make a small rectangular block of marzipan to fit in the base of the basket, then build up the sides, securing them with sugar glue. Trim the pieces to fit exactly as you assemble the box. A tiny sandwich box can be made the same way, but without the block of marzipan.

Plates

Roll out the marzipan and cut out plates using the wide end of a piping tube (tip). Mark the centre with a small round cutter.

Cups

Make a small ball of marzipan and hollow out the centre with the end of a paintbrush.

Sandwiches

Roll out white marzipan thinly between two sheets of polythene. Repeat with a piece of coloured marzipan for the filling. Sandwich small squares of coloured marzipan between squares of white marzipan and cut into small triangles.

Bowl of Strawberries

Hollow a small ball of marzipan using a ball tool to make a bowl. Roll very small pieces of red marzipan for strawberries, then add small green stalks when you have placed the strawberries in the bowl.

Bottles

Roll a small cylinder of marzipan, then roll the edge of a modelling tool on the cylinder to thin the neck of the bottle. Flatten the base of the bottle. Cut out a label from thinly rolled marzipan and a small circle for the stopper. Attach both to the bottle and paint the label with diluted paste food colouring.

Tablecloth and Napkins

Cut out a square of thinly rolled marzipan for the cloth and ruffle its edges slightly. Cut and fold tiny squares of paste for the napkins.

Completing the Cake

Place the caravan on the cake and assemble the characters in their respective positions. Add their hats and picnic accessories. Trim the board edge with ribbon.

TEMPLATES

Christening Crib, see page 74

ENLARGE TEMPLATES BY 137% ON A PHOTOCOPIER

Drape for crib

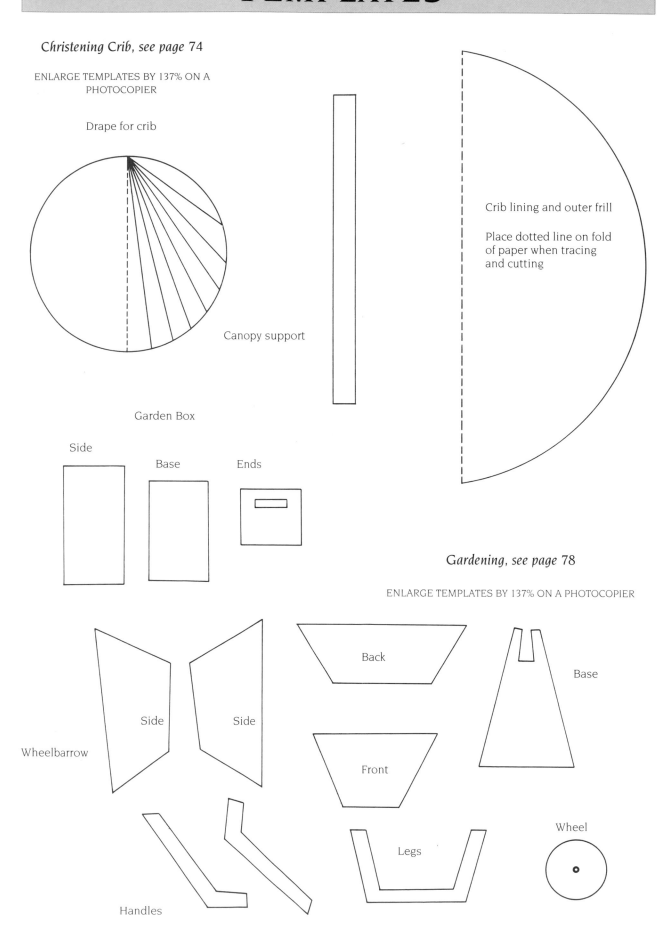

Canopy support

Crib lining and outer frill

Place dotted line on fold of paper when tracing and cutting

Garden Box

Side

Base

Ends

Gardening, see page 78

ENLARGE TEMPLATES BY 137% ON A PHOTOCOPIER

Back

Base

Side

Side

Front

Wheelbarrow

Legs

Wheel

Handles

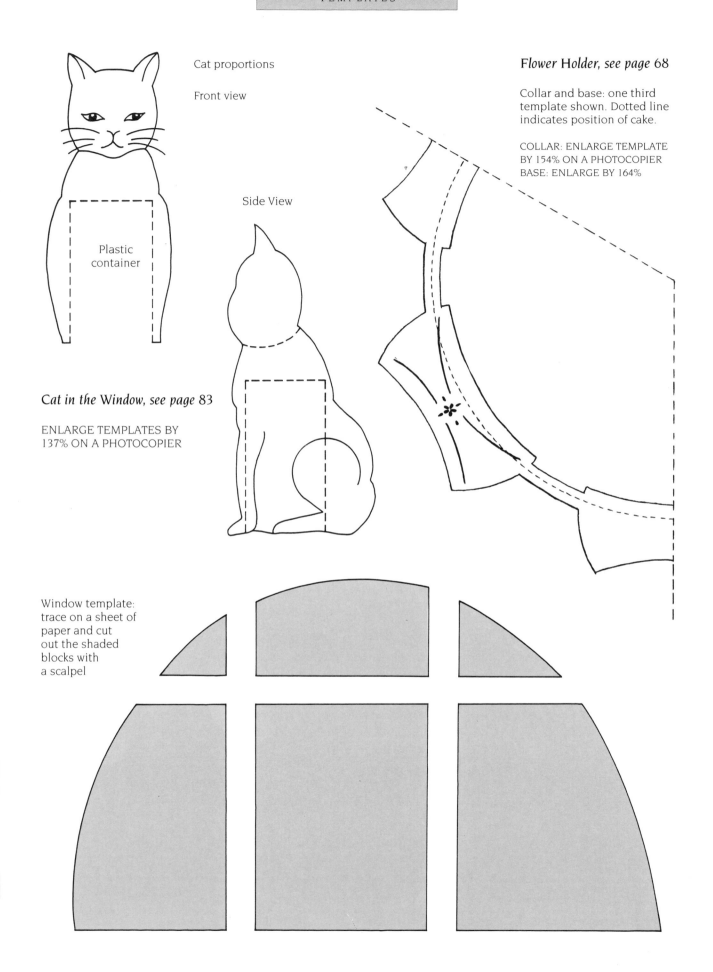

Cat proportions

Front view

Side View

Plastic
container

Cat in the Window, see page 83

ENLARGE TEMPLATES BY
137% ON A PHOTOCOPIER

Flower Holder, see page 68

Collar and base: one third
template shown. Dotted line
indicates position of cake.

COLLAR: ENLARGE TEMPLATE
BY 154% ON A PHOTOCOPIER
BASE: ENLARGE BY 164%

Window template:
trace on a sheet of
paper and cut
out the shaded
blocks with
a scalpel

Christmas Eve, see page 94

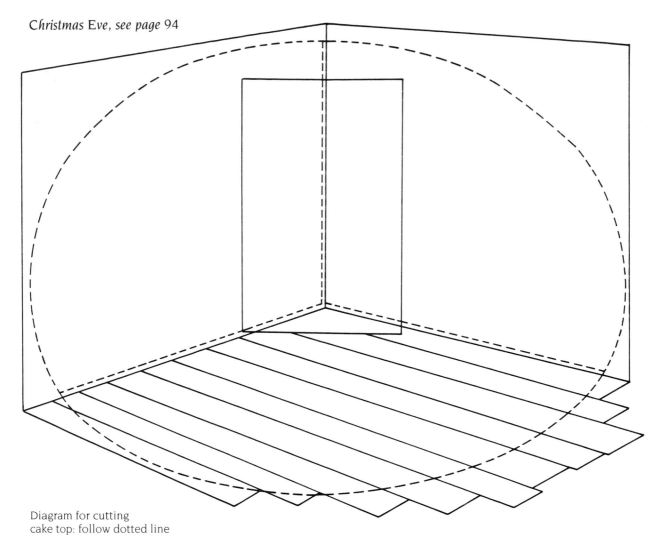

Diagram for cutting
cake top: follow dotted line

ENLARGE BY 115% ON A PHOTOCOPIER

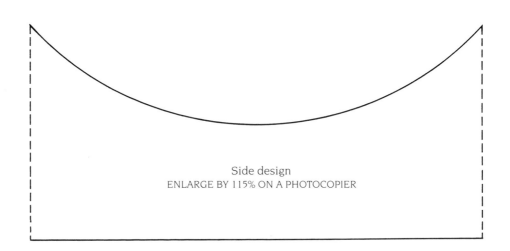

Side design
ENLARGE BY 115% ON A PHOTOCOPIER

Victoriana, see page 100

ENLARGE BY 115% ON A PHOTOCOPIER

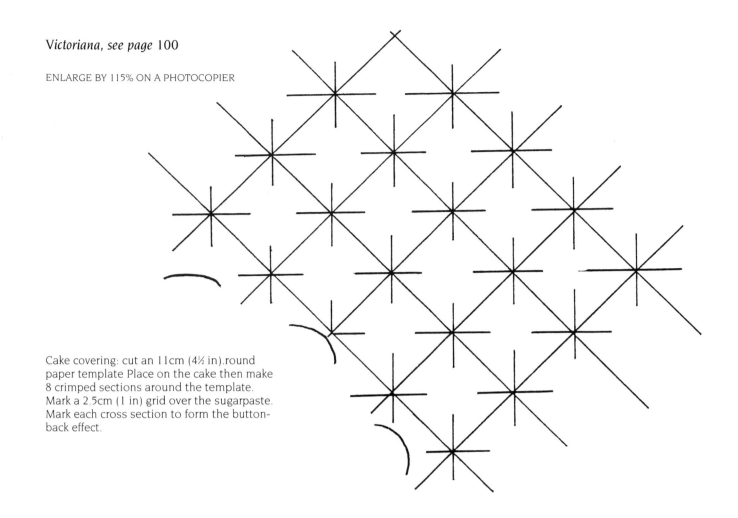

Cake covering: cut an 11cm (4½ in).round paper template Place on the cake then make 8 crimped sections around the template. Mark a 2.5cm (1 in) grid over the sugarpaste. Mark each cross section to form the button-back effect.

Christmas Eve, see page 94

TEMPLATES SHOWN FULL SIZE

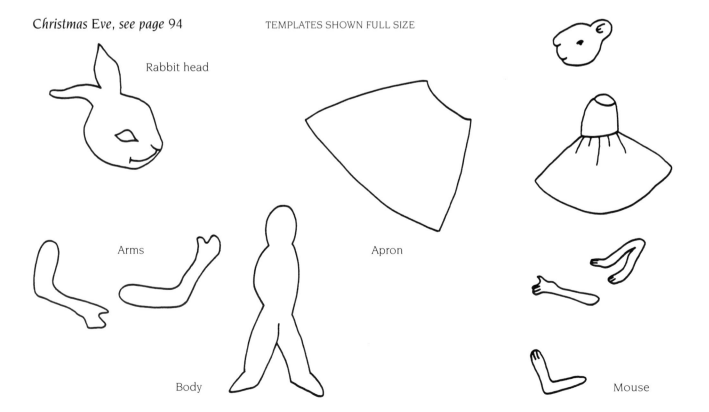

Rabbit head

Arms

Apron

Body

Mouse

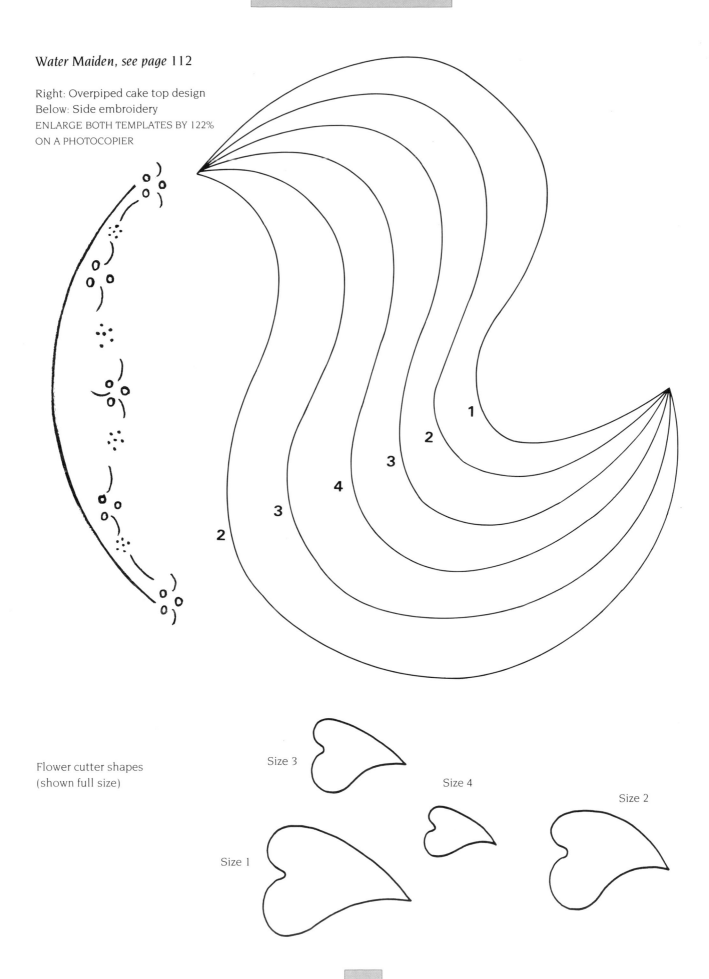

Water Maiden, see page 112

Right: Overpiped cake top design
Below: Side embroidery
ENLARGE BOTH TEMPLATES BY 122%
ON A PHOTOCOPIER

Flower cutter shapes
(shown full size)

Size 3

Size 4

Size 2

Size 1

Snow Queen, see page 123

Trace and cut out bodice
separately to make dress template

Base design:
dotted line shows position
for background and figure

ENLARGE ALL
TEMPLATES BY 137%
ON A PHOTOCOPIER

Head-dress front

Head-dress back

Background

Underarm
section

Top of arm:
shoulder
piece

Overarm section

INDEX

FOR FURTHER INFORMATION

Merehurst is the leading publisher of cake decorating books and has an excellent range of titles to suit cake decorators of all levels. Please send for a free catalogue, stating the title of this book:

United Kingdom
Marketing Department
Merehurst Ltd.
Ferry House
51 – 57 Lacy Road
London SW15 1PR
Tel: 0181 780 1177
Fax: 0181 780 1714

U.S.A./Canada
Foxwood International Ltd.
150 Nipissing Road # 6
Milton
Ontario L9T 5B2
Canada
Tel: 0101 905 875 4040
Fax: 0101 905 875 1668

Australia
Herron Book Distributors
91 Main Street
Kangaroo Point
Queensland 4169
Australia
Tel: 010 61 7 891 2866
Fax: 010 61 7 891 2909

Other Territories
For further information contact:
International Sales Department
at United Kingdom address.